Anna Luiza Salles Souto is deputy coordinator of the study *Brazilian Youth and Democracy: participation, spheres and public policies*. She is a sociologist and Director at Pólis – *Instituto de Estudos, Formação e Assessoria em Políticas Sociais*.

Itamar Silva is coordinator of the study *Brazilian Youth and Democracy: participation, spheres and public policies*. He is a journalist and Coordinator at Ibase – *Instituto Brasileiro de Análises Sociais e Econômicas*.

INTERNATIONAL LIBRARY OF POLITICAL STUDIES

See www.ibtauris.com/ILPS for a full list of titles

21. *Harold Wilson and Europe:*
Pursuing Britain's Membership of the
European Community
Melissa Pine
978 1 84511 470 1

22. *The Greek Idea: The Formation of*
National and Transnational Identities
Maria Koundoura
978 1 84511 487 9

23. *Conservative Suffragists:*
The Women's Vote and the Tory Party
Mitzi Auchterlonie
978 1 84511 485 5

24. *The Contested Countryside:*
Rural Politics and Land Controversy
in Modern Britain
Jeremy Burchardt and Philip Conford
(eds)
978 1 84511 715 3

25. *Liberals in Schism:*
A History of the National Liberal Party
David Dutton
978 1 84511 667 5

26. *Communist Women in Scotland:*
Red Clydeside from the Russian Revolution
to the End of the Soviet Union
Neil C. Rafeek
978 1 84511 624 8

27. *Richard Crossman and the Welfare State:*
Pioneer of Welfare Provision and Labour
Politics in Post-War Britain
Stephen Thornton
978 1 84511 848 8

28. *Reunifying Cyprus:*
The Annan Plan and Beyond
Andrekos Varnava and Hubert
Faustmann (eds)
978 1 84511 657 6

29. *An Irish Statesman and Revolutionary:*
The Nationalist and Internationalist Politics
of Sean MacBride
Elizabeth Keane
978 1 84511 125 0

30. *Flood Planning: The Politics of Water Security*
Jeroen Warner
978 1 84511 817 4

31. *Dark Crusade:*
Christian Zionism and US Foreign Policy
Clifford A. Kiracofe, Jr
978 1 84511 754 2

32. *Philosophy, Politics and Religion in British*
Democracy: Maurice Cowling and Conservatism
Robert Crowcroft, S. J. D. Green and
Richard Whiting (eds)
978 1 84511 976 8

33. *British Conservatism:*
The Philosophy and Politics of Inequality
Peter Dorey
978 1 84511 352 0

34. *Global Russia:*
Eurasianism, Putin and the New Right
Dmitry V. Shlapentokh
978 1 84885 036 1

35. *The Path to Devolution and Change:*
A Political History of Scotland Under
Margaret Thatcher
David Stewart
978 1 84511 938 6

36. *Democracy, Citizenship and Youth: Towards*
Social and Political Participation in Brazil
Itamar Silva and Anna Luiza Salles Souto
(eds)
978 1 84885 048 4

37. *Choosing Slovakia:*
Slavic Hungary, the Czechoslovak
Language and Accidental Nationalism
Alexander Maxwell
978 1 84885 074 3

38. *Khatami and Gorbachev: Politics of Change*
in the Islamic Republic of Iran and the USSR
Zhand Shakibi
978 1 84885 139 9

39. *Critical Turns in Critical Theory:*
New Directions in Social and Political Thought
Séamus Ó Tuama (ed.)
978 1 84511 559 3

DEMOCRACY, CITIZENSHIP AND YOUTH

Towards Social and Political Participation in Brazil

TAURIS ACADEMIC STUDIES
an imprint of
I.B.Tauris Publishers
LONDON • NEW YORK

International Development Research Centre
Ottawa • Cairo • Dakar • Montevideo • Nairobi • New Delhi • Singapore

Published in 2009 by Tauris Academic Studies
An imprint of I.B.Tauris & Co Ltd
6 Salem Road, London W2 4BU
www.ibtauris.com

Distributed in the United States and Canada exclusively
by Palgrave Macmillan, New York NY 10010

A copublication with the International Development Research Centre
PO Box 8500, Ottawa, ON, Canada K1G 3H9
info@idrc.ca / www.idrc.ca
ISBN (e-book) 978-1-55250-431-4

Copyright © 2009 International Development Research Centre

The right of Anna Luiza Salles Souto and Itamar Silva to be identified
as editor of this work has been asserted by the author in accordance with
the Copyright, Designs and Patent Act 1988.

All rights reserved. Except for brief quotations in a review, this book, or
any part thereof, may not be reproduced, stored in or introduced into a
retrieval system, or transmitted, in any form or by any means, electronic,
mechanical, photocopying, recording or otherwise, without the prior
written permission of the publisher.

International Library of Political Studies 36

ISBN 978-1-84885-048-4

A full CIP record for this book is available from the British Library
A full CIP record for this book is available from the Library of Congress

Library of Congress catalog card: available

Dialoguing: An Ibase-IDRC publication
Support: Canadian Policy Research Networks (CPRN)
International Development Research Centre (IDRC), Ottawa, Canada.
Editing in Portuguese: Flávia Mattar
English Translation: Peter Lenny MCIL
Revision: James Jude Mulholland
Graphic design and layout: Doble clic · Editoras
Revision of English Edition: Laura Pallares

Printed and bound in India by Thomson Press (India)
Camera-ready copy edited and supplied by the authors

CONTENTS

TABLES	ix
ACRONYMS	xi
FOREWORD *Regina Novaes*	xiii
RESEARCH TEAM OF THE BRAZILIAN YOUTH AND DEMOCRACY STUDY	xvii
NETWORK OF PARTNER INSTITUTIONS	xix
INTRODUCTION *Anna Luiza Salles Souto and Itamar Silva*	1
Dialogue Groups	3
Key thoughts	5
1 YOUTH AND SOCIAL PARTICIPATION IN BRAZIL: RESULTS OF A NATIONAL DIALOGUE WITH YOUNG PEOPLE IN METROPOLITAN REGIONS *Paulo Cesar Carrano*	11
Government action	13
Between work and education	16
Youth participation and schooling	17
Group participation	18

Participation in social movements	21
Perceptions on participation	23
Final remarks	27
References	29

2 SCHOOL AND YOUTH PARTICIPATION: (RE)THINKING THE LINKS 31
Juarez Tarcísio Dayrell, Geraldo Pereira Magela Leão and Nilma Lino Gomes

The socio-cultural profile of youth in the Belo Horizonte metropolitan region	33
The 'youth condition'	33
The youth condition's multiple dimensions in the BHMR	34
Social participation and youth policy	41
Perceptions of participation	42
Youth participation: some thoughts	44
School and youth participation	47
The role of schools in young people's concerns and demands	50
'Extra-curricular' activities: school at the weekends	52
Final remarks	52
References	57

3 YOUTH, INFORMATION AND EDUCATION: MEANINGS ON TELEVISION 59
Eliane Ribeiro and Patrícia Lânes

How they obtain information	62
How they understand reality	66
Beyond television	71
Final remarks	72
References	75

CONTENTS • vii

4	DEBATING THE DIALOGUE METHODOLOGY *Livia De Tommasi, Suzanne Taschereau, Nilton Bueno Fischer and Gustavo Venturi*	77
	Conversation on the Dialogues	82
	Mediating between results and public policies	104
	References	106
5	DIALOGUE DAY: YOUNG PEOPLE'S OPINIONS FORMED IN A CONTEXT OF RESEARCH AND POPULAR EDUCATION *Solange dos Santos Rodrigues*	109
	Young people evaluate Dialogue Day	110
	Young people speak out	111
	Young people extend their social networks	115
	Young people learn through the Dialogue Groups	117
	Young people thinking about Brazil	121
	Dialogics and learning, research and popular education	123
	References	128
6	BRAZIL AND CANADA: LEARNING THROUGH COLLABORATION *Mary Pat MacKinnon and Suzanne Taschereau*	131
	Introduction	132
	Context, impetus and milestones	133
	Supporting successful collaboration and shared learning: key factors	138
	Shared belief in and commitment to the role of youth in strengthening democracy	138
	Respecting and building on Brazilian experience and expertise	138
	Bringing together theory and practice: policy, researchers and practitioners	139
	Building relationships and trust	140
	Dialogue challenges in Brazil and how they were addressed	141

How this collaboration influenced
CPRN's dialogue with youth ... 145
 Engaging youth in issue identification and
 dialogue planning ... 145
 Youth in leadership roles ... 146
 Beyond the research report: building
 commitment to action ... 147
Successes and reflections ... 148
 Process and policy outcomes ... 148
 New networks leverage action ... 149
 Reflections on moving forward ... 149

7 Networked Research:
A Decentralized, Participatory Study ... 155
Sebastião Soares

The logic of the network's structure and functioning ... 159

Indispensable periodic workshops ... 161

Collective construction ... 163

The network ... 165
 Overall Project Coordination ... 165
 Technical and financial support ... 167
 Technical and methodological support ... 167

Final remarks ... 176

8 Brazilian Youth and Democracy:
The Press Campaign ... 179
Rogério Pacheco Jordão

Defining a strategy ... 180

Step-by-step ... 181

Results ... 182

Ibase's review Democracia Viva ... 184

 TV and alternative media ... 184

Notes ... 187

Index ... 193

TABLES

Chapter 1: Youth and Social Participation in Brazil

1. Participation in groups by sex, age group and class (percentage) — 19
2. Participation in movements to improve neighbourhood / city conditions (percentage) — 21

Chapter 3: Youth, Information and Education

1. Sources and media used by young people to stay informed (percentage –multiple responses) — 63
2. Young people's participation in media, by social class (percentage) — 65
3. Young people who correctly answered the meaning of selected acronyms and expressions (percentage) — 67
4. Young people who answered the definition of acronyms and expressions correctly, by source or medium where they obtain information (percentage) — 71

Chapter 6: Brazil and Canada

1. Collaboration Milestones — 136

ACRONYMS

BHMR	Belo Horizonte Metropolitan Region
CPRN	Canadian Policy Research Networks
CRIA	Centro de Referência Integral de Adolescentes, Salvador, Bahia
ECA	Brazil's Statute on Children
EQUIP	Escola de Formação Quilombo dos Palmares, Recife
FTAA	Free Trade Area of the Americas
IBASE	Instituto Brasileiro de Análises Sociais e Economicas
IBGE	Brazilian Institute of Geography and Statistics
IDRC	International Development Research Center, Canadá
INESC	Instituto de Estudos Socioeconômicos, Brasilia
ISER	Instituto de Estudos, Formação e Assessoria em Políticas Sociais, Rio de Janeiro
PÓLIS	Instituto de Estudos de Formacão e Assessoria em Politicas Sociais
UFF	Universidade Federal Fluminense, Rio de Janeiro
UFMG	Universidade Federal de Minas Gerais
UFRGS	Universidade Federal do Rio Grande do Sul
UN	United Nations Organization
UNIPOP	Instituto Universidade Popular, Belém, Pará

FOREWORD

This book is the result of a process hitherto unheard of in Brazil. A short time ago, it would have not been considered possible to produce information on Brazilian youth that draws on rigorous academic research, militant commitment by non-governmental organisations nationally renowned for their part in the struggle for participatory democracy, support from a Canadian international cooperation organisation offering not only funding, but a valuable interchange of methodology and, lastly, support and real interest from the Brazilian federal government. The project was also unprecedented in another way. Throughout the course of the research, a 'political council' accompanied the process by offering suggestions and input and, most importantly, sharing the results with a broad, diverse public.

There are two more important reasons that the study underpinning this book should be highly valued. Firstly, a network of partner institutions throughout Brazil's vast territory was successfully put together for the study. Secondly, the research made a timely contribution to building Brazil's National Youth Policy. This last point calls for some important clarifications.

In Brazil, it was not until the late 1990s that the discussion on youth policies gained momentum. It was a time marked by rapid and far-reaching technological change, which transformed the labour market and spawned various forms of violence, heightening feelings of insecurity among young people. In that context, researchers, international organizations, social movements, municipal and state policy-makers directed vigorous effort to uncovering the unique features of this generation's social experience by identifying its vulnerabilities, demands and potentials.

One prominent initiative in 2003 was *Projeto Juventude*, carried out by *Instituto Cidadania*. It conducted a wide-ranging national survey, held conversations with youth movements, experts and non-governmental organizations and organized several regional seminars as well as one at the national level.

Also in 2003, Congress set up the first-ever parliamentary commission on youth policies. The commission held public hearings all over Brazil, called a national conference in Brasilia, and organized visits abroad to tap into related international experience. In the process, a constitutional amendment, a National Youth Plan and a Youth Statute were drafted.

In 2004, an inter-ministerial group to examine government youth programmes and measures, was set up at the request of Brazil's president, Luiz Inacio Lula da Silva, and the Minister of the General Secretariat of the Presidency, Luiz Dulci. This group, with representatives from nineteen ministries, diagnosed the situation of Brazil's youth. Additionally it recommended inter-ministerial integration and shared management of programmes and actions, which are basic requirements for constituting a national youth policy.

Between June and September 2004, the results from these and other initiatives reached the Presidency of the Republic. All converged on one point: the need to set up an institutional space specifically for 'youth'. That was the next step. In dialogue with local actors while also taking international experience into account, the Lula government was able to design its National Youth Policy. On 1 February 2005, a provisional order was sent to Congress, where it was approved with the support of members from a range of political parties. Finally, the law was put into force by the President in July that same year. Today, all young Brazilians between the ages of 15 and 29 are potential beneficiaries of this policy.

The law instituted the National Youth Secretariat (*Secretaria Nacional de Juventude*, SNJ), which reports to the Secretariat-General of the Presidency of the Republic and whose main task is to coordinate and supervise programmes and measures for young people; the National Youth Council (*Conselho Nacional da Juventude, Conjuve*), an advisory board responsible for fostering studies and proposing guidelines; and the National Youth Inclusion Programme (*Programa Nacional de Inclusão de Jovens, ProJovem*), an emergency programme for 18 to 24 year olds excluded from both school and the labour market.

The purpose of this preface is to highlight the timely historical circumstances that have led to the results of the study (conducted by Ibase, Pólis and IDRC) being immediately used to inform the design and introduction of youth policies in Brazil.

The National Youth Council was set in place by President Lula in August 2005. At this council, the results of the quantitative study and the outcomes of the Dialogue Groups informed not only the council members on the part of civil society – including Ibase and other participants in the *Juventude Brasileira e Democracia* – but also government representatives, enabling them all to participate more fully.

To research and produce knowledge about youth, and all of its inequalities and diversities, is to contribute to its political recognition as a public stakeholder, with demands, languages and creativity of its own. This is also the aim of this book. The authors are confident that the avenues of social dialogue can be renewed and broadened.

Certainly much remains to be done. We are just beginning. However, due credit must be given for the steps taken thus far. The study *Juventude Brasileira e Democracia* is without a doubt a successful experience in knowledge production that is having a beneficial influence on ongoing social processes. By acknowledging youth as the 'subject of rights', hopefully new ways and ground-breaking paths forward for a more just and democratic society will be encountered. With the same view to innovation, we hope that this book will help continue and extend this rich and challenging dialogue among social organizations and researchers from Brazil and Canada.

Regina Novaes
Member of the Political Council of the
Juventude e Democracia study,
Chair of the Conselho Nacional de Juventude (Conjuve),
National Deputy Secretary for Youth

RESEARCH TEAM OF THE BRAZILIAN YOUTH AND DEMOCRACY STUDY

Coordinator: **Itamar Silva (Ibase)**
Deputy coordinator: **Anna Luiza Salles Souto (Pólis)**
Technical coordinator: **Sebastião José Martins Soares (Ibase)**
Technical team
Eliane Ribeiro
Patrícia Lânes
Paulo Cesar Carrano
Statistics advisors
Coordinator: Marco Antônio Aguiar
Leonardo Méllo
Márcia Tibau
Study network
Supervisors by metropolitan region
Ana Paula de Oliveira Corti – São Paulo, Juarez Tarcísio Dayrell – Belo Horizonte, Júlia Tais Campos Ribeiro – Salvador, Livia de Tommasi – Recife, Lúcia Isabel da Conceição Silva – Belém, Nilton Bueno Fischer – Porto Alegre, Ozanira Ferreira da Costa – Federal District, and Solange dos Santos Rodrigues – Rio de Janeiro.

Assistants by metropolitan region
Alexandre da Silva Aguiar – Rio de Janeiro, Ana Paula Carvalho Silva – Salvador, Carmem Zeli Vargas Gil Souza – Porto Alegre, Elisabete Regina Baptista de Oliveira – São Paulo, Fernanda Glória França Colaço – Salvador, Francisca Guiomar Cruz da Silva – Belém, Geraldo Pereira Magela Leão – Belo Horizonte, Graça Elenice dos Santos Braga – Recife, Karina Aparecida Figueiredo – Federal District, Marcílio

Dantas Brandão – Recife, Marilena Cunha – Rio de Janeiro, Nara Vieira Ramos – Porto Alegre, Nilda Stecanela – Porto Alegre, Nilma Lino Gomes – Belo Horizonte, Perla Ribeiro – Federal District, Raquel Souza dos Santos – São Paulo, Rosely Risuenho Viana – Belém, Sueli Salva – Porto Alegre.

Intern researchers
André Araújo – Salvador, Andréia Rosalina Silva – Belo Horizonte, Antonio Elba – Recife, Bianca Brandão – Rio de Janeiro, Bruno Nazarebo Ribeiro da Silva – Belém, Carolina Ruoso – Recife, Clara Belato – Rio de Janeiro, Cristiane Santos – Salvador, Daniele Monteiro – Rio de Janeiro, Eduardo Assunção Rocha – Porto Alegre, Elaine Bezerra – Recife, Elizângela Menezes – Federal District, Érica Pessanha – São Paulo, Germana de Castro – Recife, Gustavo Barhuch Píscaro de Carvalho – Belo Horizonte, Janisse Carvalho – Distrito Federal, Juan Pablo Diehl Severo – Porto Alegre, Juliana Batista dos Reis – Belo Horizonte, Juliana de Souza – Porto Alegre, Leila Pimenta – Salvador, Lorena Marques – Federal District, Luciene Aviz – Belém, Marcela Moraes – São Paulo, Márcio Amaral – Porto Alegre, Mariana Camacho – Rio de Janeiro, Melissa de Carvalho Farias – Porto Alegre, Nilton Lopes – Salvador, Priscila Bastos – Rio de Janeiro, Rachel Quintiliano – São Paulo, Rafael Madeira – Distrito Federal, Raimundo Jairo Barroso Cardoso – Belém, Sarah Daniele Bahia da Silva – Belém, Shirley Pereira Raimundo – Belo Horizonte, Viviane Nebó – São Paulo, and Viviane Paliarini – Porto Alegre.

Secretaries
Inês Carvalho
Rozi Billo

NETWORK OF PARTNER INSTITUTIONS

Instituto Brasileiro de Análises Sociais e Econômicas (Ibase)/ Rio de Janeiro, RJ

Instituto de Estudos, Formação e Assessoria em Políticas Sociais (Pólis)/ São Paulo, SP

Iser Assessoria/Rio de Janeiro, RJ

Observatório Jovem do Rio de Janeiro – Universidade Federal Fluminense/Niterói, RJ

Observatório da Juventude da Universidade Federal de Minas Gerais/ Belo Horizonte, MG

Ação Educativa – Assessoria, Pesquisa e Informação/São Paulo, SP

Universidade Federal do Rio Grande do Sul (UFRGS)/Porto Alegre, RS

Instituto de Estudos Socioeconômicos (Inesc)/Brasília, DF

Centro de Referência Integral de Adolescentes (Cria)/Salvador, BA

Instituto Universidade Popular (Unipop)/Belém, PA

Escola de Formação Quilombo dos Palmares (Equip)/Recife, PE

International Development Research Centre (IDRC)/Canada

Canadian Policy Research Networks (CPRN)/Canada

INTRODUCTION

Anna Luiza Salles Souto*
Itamar Silva

'The individual who opens up to the world and to others, and with that gesture inaugurates the dialogic relationship finds confirmation in restlessness and curiosity, as well as inconclusiveness in the permanent movement of history.'

(Paulo Freire 1997)

The *Instituto Brasileiro de Análises Sociais e Econômicas* (Ibase) and the *Instituto de Estudos, Formação e Assessoria em Políticas Sociais* (Pólis) are pleased to present this collection of thinking on youth and research methodology procedures. Its goal is to have a qualitative influence on policy-making in order to help extend rights and opportunities for young Brazilians.

The thinking provided in this book corroborates the view that the life experiences of new generations in different parts

---

* About the authors:
Anna Luiza Salles Souto is deputy coordinator of the study *Brazilian Youth and Democracy: participation, spheres and public policies*. She is a sociologist and Director at Pólis – *Instituto de Estudos, Formação e Assessoria em Políticas Sociais*.
Itamar Silva is coordinator of the study *Brazilian Youth and Democracy: participation, spheres and public policies*. He is a journalist and Coordinator at Ibase – *Instituto Brasileiro de Análises Sociais e Econômicas*.

of the world, although they may be interpreted in extremely singular manners (by social class, colour/ethnicity, gender, religion, culture and so on), contain some essentially universal elements. That is to say, they necessarily reflect the new global panoramas and their consequences and repercussions in the interconnected world we live in.

Our goal is to share our data and analysis from this exercise with other countries and continents. Through this sharing, we hope to prompt ideas about new, more sensitive, rapid, and effective research methods which can address what is diverse, what is singular and what is universal. Above all, this research yields findings and discoveries that can *denaturalize* social injustices, not just for young Brazilians, but for the vast population of poor youth seeking better conditions of life in a profoundly unequal world.

For this purpose, the extensive network of Brazilian and Canadian partners involved in this undertaking agreed that the first task was to learn to listen to young people, to understand the conditions they live in, their similarities and differences, and their outlooks on the enormous challenges posed by present-day societies. The body of thinking presented here is the result of the study *Juventude Brasileira e Democracia: participação, esferas públicas e políticas* (*Brazilian Youth and Democracy: Participation, Spheres and Public Policies*), which listened to and debated with a wide variety of young Brazilians between the ages of 15 and 24. They talked not just about their realities, dreams, expectations, demands, needs and wishes, but also about the limits on, and scope for, participation in political, social and community activities.

The study was carried out between 2004 and 2006 in seven of Brazil's metropolitan regions (Rio de Janeiro, São Paulo, Recife, Salvador, Porto Alegre, Belo Horizonte and Belem) and in the Federal District (Brasilia) under the coordination of the non-governmental organizations Ibase and Pólis, with financial cooperation from Canada's International Development Research Center (IDRC) and technical collaboration from Canadian Policy Research Networks (CPRN). In order to carry out the study, an experienced network of research partners was organized. Contributions from researchers associated with research centres at various universities were brought into dialogue with researchers with civil-society organizations and groups. The network included *Instituto de Estudos, Formação e Assessoria em Políticas Sociais* (Iser Assessoria), Rio de Janeiro; *Observatório Jovem do Rio de Janeiro/Universidade Federal Fluminense*, Rio de Janeiro; *Observatório da Juventude da Universidade Federal de Minas Gerais*, Belo Horizonte, Minas Gerais; *Ação Educativa – Assessoria, Pesquisa e Informação*, São Paulo; *Universidade Federal do Rio Grande do Sul* (UFRGS), Porto Alegre, Rio Grande do Sul; *Instituto de Estudos Socioeconômicos* (Inesc), Brasilia, Distrito Federal; *Centro de Referência Integral de Adolescentes* (Cria), Salvador, Bahia; *Instituto Universidade Popular* (Unipop), Belém, Pará; and *Escola de Formação Quilombo dos Palmares* (Equip), Recife, Pernambuco.

The study was conducted using two methodological approaches.[1] The first, a statistical survey, was carried out through the use of a questionnaire which was applied to a wide-ranging population sample (8,000 young people)[2] in an effort to create a profile of the young people, their various forms of participation and their perceptions of education, work, culture and participation. The second approach was a qualitative study based on the Choice Work Dialogue Methodology ('Dialogue Groups') in which a total of 913 young people, divided into 39 groups, discussed the topics of education, work, culture/leisure and participation in depth.

Dialogue Groups

The qualitative phase of the study centred on dialogue. The key purpose of the methodology is to go beyond the logic that predominates in policy-related opinion polls, which merely record attitudes without creating opportunities for people to join together to pursue their thinking on the issues. The Dialogue Group approach assumes that we do not form opinions individually, but through interaction. During Dialogue Day, participants receive official information on the topic to be addressed and are invited to take part in an intensive discussion process among individuals of both sexes, from different social classes, age groups, places of residence and so on.

Using dialogue as a method presupposes that participants are able to listen and to interact without any particular opinion being aggressively advocated to the point of disregarding the opinion of others. The Dialogue Groups thus function simultaneously as a research method and an extended educational process. The dialogic relationship follows from openness, from baring oneself to others, from accepting oneself as permanently in the making, and permanently learning. In this study, the Dialogue Group methodology stimulated the young people to speak from their life contexts and to interact with the topics proposed (education, work, culture/leisure and participation). On that basis, consensuses were built up when possible and significant differences were explicitly brought out. All of the material collected during the meetings was analyzed in depth.

One of the most important and innovative aspects of the study was the fruitful North-South interchange among institutions in Canada and Brazil, which proved a valuable field for joint learning. North-South cooperation was taken beyond the economic dimension, which limits cooperation to the endeavour of integrating markets. This cooperation was guided from the outset by the educational, scientific and cultural meaning of bringing countries and cultures closer together in a process of permanent dialogue, which opened up new possibilities for consolidating cooperation that embodies the principles of sovereignty, solidarity and respect for diversity.

The exchange between CPRN and the institutions involved in the study (the coordinating body and the organizations that carried out the study in the various regions of Brazil) deserves special attention. It proved to be a mutual learning process that should go on record.

Organizing the research in network form among nine local institutions (non-governmental organizations and public universities) not only proved appropriate for undertaking the work, it also constituted a valuable field for building methodologies and analyses together.

Another aspect of the study is the diffusion of study results in the local and national press. The strategy used made it possible to sensitize the media and to draw attention to data which shows that young people are the subjects of rights, and capable of critical thinking and of making constructive proposals about their lives.

Key thoughts

This book presents the research process and outcomes in eight chapters written by leading specialists on youth. They are researchers and journalists associated with a range of universities and non-governmental organizations in Brazil and Canada.

The variety of outlooks and issues conveyed in this book, as well as the insight with which they have been produced, illustrates well how important it is to conduct additional research in this field. Understanding the social space currently reserved for young people is fundamental to constructing arguments that can strongly contribute to the social inclusion of youth by instituting measures to integrate this portion of the population into social-promotion networks (education, work, culture, communication and so on). Such inclusion is crucial to bringing sustainability to democracy and to reducing inequalities, particularly in Latin America.

The first three chapters offer re-readings of the research data. The first, *Youth and Social Participation in Brazil: Results of a National Dialogue with Young People in Metropolitan Regions*, is written by Paulo Cesar Carrano, a member of the project's technical team. It examines key issues that emerged from the data collected in the two stages – the opinion poll and the Dialogue Groups – particularly work, education and young people's group activities.

The starting assumption is that the nature of social participation – its intensity, quality, quantity, scope and social, cultural and political meanings – correlates largely with life conditions and the structure of opportunities that society provides to young people of various ages. The chapter considers the efforts that young people with differing identity profiles (in terms of class, gender, colour/race, place of residence) make to surmount obstacles to participation.

Next, Juarez Tarcísio Dayrell, Geraldo Leão and Nilma Lino Gomes, the team responsible for the study in the Belo Horizonte metropolitan region in Minas Gerais in south-eastern Brazil, present the chapter *School and Youth Participation: (Re)thinking the Links*. Building on the quantitative and qualitative data, they explore the problems – from the point of view of young people – of how schools act to create the necessary conditions to permit and encourage youth participation. It questions how far the model of school organization and its dynamics produce an environment conducive to developing experience in participation, given the diversity of the youth in Brazil.

Rounding off the set of data analyses generated by the study, the third chapter *Youth, Information and Education: Meanings on Television*, is written by Eliane Ribeiro Andrade and Patrícia Lânes, both members of the core team. The authors build on a set of figures that highlight tensions in relationships among information, education and the media.

The focus is on television since of the 85.8 per cent of young people who said they try to stay informed about what is happening in the world, 84.5 per cent said television was their source of information. The authors try to understand the relationship between the means that young people report using to stay informed about 'things happening in the world' and what they answer when asked the meaning of a group of acronyms and expressions reflecting various political demands. In order to understand to what point television has played a preponderant role in these young people's worldview, they draw a first approximation between information and education.

The following chapters examine the study methodologies, process and its implementation. In Chapter Four, *Debating the Dialogue Methodology*, Livia De Tommasi and Nilton Fischer, who supervised the study in the Recife and Porto Alegre metropolitan regions respectively, debate with Brazilian sociologist, Gustavo Venturi, and the study's methodological advisor, Suzanne Tascherau. The authors discuss the challenges raised by the Choice Work Dialogue ('Dialogue Group') Methodology. They explore the potential, challenges and difficulties of this methodological resource in the light of the project's experience while considering the contributions of research methodology specialist Gustavo Venturi.

Next, the study supervisor for the Rio de Janeiro metropolitan region, Solange Rodrigues, examines how young people viewed the educational endeavour of the Dialogue Group methodology. In the chapter *Dialogue Day: Young People's Opinions Formed in a Context of Research and Popular Education*, she takes one of the methodology's key components as her starting point: the assumption that access to information and dialogue can be essential to forming well-grounded, considered opinions.

By examining young people's answers to the question 'What was most important in what happened here today?' at the end of the Dialogue Group, the author presents a set of youth perceptions from different regions of Brazil. What stands out among these perceptions is that the young people saw the Dialogue Groups as moments when they were able to express their opinions, and they appreciated having their ideas heard and taken into consideration. They also saw the groups as an opportunity to meet new people, which enabled them to recognize a shared identity. Another aspect they valued was the *learning process*.

The chapter *Brazil and Canada: Learning through Collaboration*, written by Mary Pat MacKinnon, director of CPRN, and Suzanne Taschereau, addresses the process and results of the rich collaboration among several Brazilian NGOs, CPRN and IDRC. Motivated by a shared commitment to strengthen democracies through the meaningful engagement of young people, the partners contributed their knowledge, experience and passion to produce a credible process and product.

Recounting the key milestones and elements of this collaboration, the authors explore the challenges which were addressed, identify factors that contributed to the project's success, share their learning and reflect on what is needed to advance the theory and practice of public dialogue (with particular reference to young people) in Canada and Brazil. The chapter concludes by asking questions and reflecting on how to best advance collaboration on international research and practice. More specifically it also addresses how to sharpen methodologies and results and the impacts of deliberative processes.

The two final chapters examine how this networked study was constructed and conducted and how the dynamics of communication (press strategies, publicity mechanisms and so on) operate in a research process. The chapter called *Networked Research: A Decentralized, Participatory Study*, was written by Sebastião Soares, the study's technical coordinator. It addresses three dimensions of this networked endeavour: the reason for setting up a network of organizations to conduct the study, including a balance of the risks and gains of this option; the logic on how the network functioned, including a description of the stages in setting up this organizational arrangement and the resources used during the research to bring it to a successful conclusion; and lastly, the network itself, its participants and some of the results it yielded.

In the final chapter, *Brazilian Youth and Democracy: The Press Campaign*, journalist Rogério Jordão analyzes the role of communication in publicizing the study. He describes the media response to the results, highlighting the importance of an integrated approach to thinking about communications (involving partners, NGOs, press and so on), and how best to use the media in building democracy in information.

Finally, the thinking and analyses presented in this publication join existing knowledge about Brazilian and international – particularly Latin American – youth, thereby broadening the debate, influencing youth policies, and fostering stronger support and opportunity networks to enable youth in all of its diversity to envisage *another possible world*.

The dialogue is open!

Chapter 1

YOUTH AND SOCIAL PARTICIPATION IN BRAZIL

Results of a National Dialogue with Young People in Metropolitan Regions

*Paulo Cesar Carrano**

The study *Brazilian Youth and Democracy: Participation, Spheres and Public Policies* asked young people aged 15 to 24 from seven metropolitan regions[1] and the Federal District about their willingness to 'participate'. It also examined the dynamics set up by these young people when they take on an active role in pursuing certain 'paths to participation'. This includes paths directed to broadening their right to live their youth more fully and to improving conditions of life in Brazil. These two intentions framed the opinion polls and Dialogue Groups carried out in the course of 2005.

The main motivation behind the study was to build a body of evidence that could animate youth advocacy groups and contribute to the development of youth policies in Brazil.

---

* Paulo Cesar Carrano Ph.D. was on the technical team of the study *Juventude Brasileira e Democracia: participação, esferas públicas e políticas*. Professor at Universidade Federal Fluminense (UFF), he also coordinates the youth observatory *Observatório Jovem do Rio de Janeiro*/UFF and is a CNPq researcher.

Accordingly, the key avenues of research consisted of asking young people about their main public demands in the areas of education, work and culture, and questioning them about their predisposition towards involvement in participatory social processes oriented towards securing rights.

The study produced significant data and stimulated debate on the challenge of participating to build democracy in Brazil. By revisiting data from the survey, which polled 8,000 young people, this chapter discusses of the importance of youth participation.

When talking about youth participation, it is important to bear in mind the multiple factors that stand as objective and subjective barriers to entry by young people. These barriers are related to youth being situated in the unstable sociological field that precedes their finding placement in social and productive structures. Youth can no longer be considered tutored children nor are they socially and economically emancipated adults; they are individuals being educated under special conditions. The period of youth can be considered decisive in constructing values and constituting adult subjectivities oriented to a greater or lesser extent towards civic participation.

Although one should not think deterministically, social and political participation is intimately related to life situation. The social and economic difficulties facing most of Brazil's youth act directly to heighten their sensation of insecurity about the present and the future. The situation of increasing instability and despair at the incapacity of the State to promote rights, social well-being and security is a major hindrance to developing citizenship and youth participation. Additionally, the historical, systemic inequality of Brazilian society undermines the family's ability to assure young people the objective conditions necessary to lend quality to their youth experience. This is a phenomenon that is extremely damaging to the transition to adult life.

This context of inequality and diversity is nonetheless traversed by threads which are common to this generation and which give a certain unity to being young at this point in history. In addition to sharing cultural identities and aesthetic expressions, there are other things in common: the experience of the same (accelerated) *techno-scientific-informational* pace of life (Santos 1994); increasing possibilities for choosing paths in the interplay of constructing one's own *self* (Melucci 2004), rather than just following the path laid out by the family; greater sexual freedom; having to cope with the distress – in some cases, real anguish – of being unable to think about or predict a future of work and happiness realistically and with any degree of precision; and living on a day-to-day basis in fear of violence that is no longer something distant affecting 'others', but the ever-present possibility of death, pain, humiliation or material loss. There is, nonetheless, something that this generation has in common and must be recognized which is the unequal distribution of liberties, needs and violence in a society divided into social classes, as well as other inequalities relating to gender condition and skin colour.

We believe that public policies directed at Brazilian youth must be developed based on a realistic perception of this societal situation.

Government action

Youth policies in Brazil focus prominently on two types of intervention, which vary according to how youth is conceived. One sees youth as a social threat, while the other recognises young people as the subjects of rights.

The former concept results in coercive policies to control the threat and 'protect' society from youth. The latter, which is more unusual, reflects the perception of young people as socially active subjects who face social problems that bring instability to this phase of life (Carrano & Sposito 2003). Another approach is to be found between these two extremes. It is directed to young people in situations of risk or social vulnerability, and represents a whole generation of public measures strongly connected with the sphere of social assistance.

Krauskopf (2005) argues that youth policy orientations in Latin America run from the traditional and reductionist through to a new generation of 'advanced' policies. The latter consider youth to be a strategic development stakeholder and no longer a 'problem phase' or 'subjects in preparation' as in the former two approaches. A new rhetoric – adopted by international development agencies, governments and social organizations – calls for the adoption of a generational approach with new collaborating relationships between young people and adults. This approach considers young people to be the active subjects of policies and strategic stakeholders in development.

A significant field of research can be set up around understanding the forms and content which organize young subjects' personal and collective practices in constituting their public space. It is in this context that research into the opportunities for young people and the scope for them to influence and legitimize public decisions that affect them gains importance academically and for democracy.

The creation of agencies to foster youth policies is a relatively recent phenomenon in Brazil – and, generally speaking, has not amounted to government policy. Rather, public policies and agencies directed to Brazil's youth population have constituted a fragile institutional fabric with little political prestige within the machinery of government at all levels of the Federation (municipal, state and federal).

Youth policies in Brazil have shown signs of a shift away from the 'problem approach' of combating violence and controlling young people's free time, to assuring their rights.

Brazil also seems to be witnessing what León (2003) called the 'aggregate programme concept' when analyzing policies in Chile during the 1990s, which refers to the sum total of programmes and projects without any mediation by effective, integrated public policies. In this context, actions directed to youth oscillate between 'educational modernization', 'social control', 'problem youth', 'human capital' or even the new, 'advanced' paradigms – that have yet to be applied in practice – which consider young people to be 'subjects of rights' or 'strategic development stakeholders'.

Over the past decade initiatives have been taken in Brazil to bring public policy makers closer to urban youth in an endeavour to incorporate the latter's demands for rights. These measures have set up municipal youth forums, participatory youth budgets, opinion polls, inventories or 'mappings' of culture groups, informal meetings between policy makers and organized groups and, more recently, have given rise to youth councils at the municipal, state and national levels.

During the first Lula administration (2002-06), bodies such as the National Youth Secretariat and the National Youth Council were set up at the federal level. The Legislative power has also brought in parliamentary commissions devoted to organizing specific plans and laws directed to youth. However, to discuss the foolishness of most of these measures is beyond the scope of this chapter.

To paraphrase Oscar León (*op. cit.*) when he speaks of youth policies in Chile, we may not yet have a 'lost decade' in Brazilian youth policies, but the last five years have certainly been a painful trial-and-error learning process. The reiterated public discourse that asserts the need for young people to be active, participating subjects in the policies directed at them makes it worth mentioning.

The visibility of cultural youth groups has led youth policy makers to seek dialogue with these actors, who are bringing a new meaning and practice of collective action into the public administration. By and large, however, the initiatives that seek to expand youth participation in government actions and policies for young people must face a lack of social and political participation by most young Brazilians. Therefore, surveys of youth participation, and its restrictions and potentials, can broaden our understanding of the social processes that truly form part of young people's lives.

Between work and education

The study, which was directed mainly at young Brazilians' potential for participation and the forms and content of their participation, showed that the greater the degree of schooling and family income, the greater the likelihood of involvement in associative practices. The opinion poll revealed that youth with the most schooling participates most in groups. However, it also demonstrated that advancing age coincides with a decline in stimuli and conditions conducive to group activities.

For most young people, low income levels and consumption capacity require that they look for work as a condition for subsisting and meeting material and symbolic needs. This distinguishes a particular manner of experiencing one's youth. It cannot be identified with what is usually taken for granted as the right to live the 'social moratorium' (Margulis & Urresti 1996), which entitles youth the freedom from the need to work, in order to devote themselves to training, study, and group and leisure activities.

The process of seeking and finding employment is an uncertain one, especially for young people from poorer families. This portion of youth finds itself occupying whatever jobs are offered, which are mostly precarious and unprotected and afford little or no opportunity to embark or advance on a professional career. Informality grows as one descends the strata of income and consumption. Academic achievement generally coincides with greater likelihood of finding formal employment, which is decisive for young people, given that unemployment among youth in Brazil is three times higher than among the overall population.

Youth participation and schooling

In Brazil, quality indicators in fundamental[2] and middle schools are increasingly tending downward, most intensely in the public education system. Regional and interregional inequalities in basic material needs are mirrored in differential access to, and length of, schooling, as well as in access to culture and leisure facilities and the information media, especially computers and the Internet. This constitutes the contemporary expression of the historical exclusion of the poor – particularly those on the periphery of the system – from the benefits of science and technology in societies based on the capitalist mode of production.

Better access conditions to information and cultural goods, along with better schooling, place upper-class youth in a better position to participate socially, culturally and politically. The study indicates that participation in student activities, for example, is quantitatively greater among strata representing wealthier and better-schooled youth. With respect to poor youth's relationship with school, one can see a marked disconnect between age and grade. This demonstrates the intermittent attendance of those who manage to reach middle school, as they are failed, leave and return to school. We must remember that access to the highest levels of education is a key to broader social participation opportunities and also to engagement and learning connected with the institutions of learning themselves.

In addition to the difficulties in accessing and staying in school, young people also face a situation in which public institutions predominantly offer what is considered uninteresting curricular content. Schools figure as institutions that are not very open to creating spaces and situations that favour social, solidarity, public debate and cultural experience or formative curricular or extra-curricular activities. The study revealed a perception that schools do not make room for, nor do they stimulate, the formation of basic habits and values that encourage youth participation. That fact is more problematic for poor youth for whom school is practically the only institution through which they gain access to these symbolic goods.

With respect to information technology, foreign languages, sports, arts and preparatory courses for university entrance, there is a new, refined educational inequality in place among young people according to their class background. In this case, once again, wealthier youth and students at private schools are favoured. Schooling is decisive in developing the habit of reading, with the data showing that young people with more schooling read more, and that public school students read less than those at private schools.

Group participation

According to the opinion poll, 28.1 per cent of young people stated that they participate in some type of group. Increasing age coincides with the decreasing likelihood of young people joining a group. The 'joining rate' is more variable, however, when young people's membership in groups is compared by social class and by years of schooling. The wealthier (classes A/B) tend to participate more (33.5 per cent); followed by class C (28.2 per cent) and then the poorer (classes D/E), with 24.0 per cent. Therefore there is a direct correlation between social class, years of schooling and group participation rates. There are no significant differences in participation by the interviewees' sex.

Table 1 – Participation in groups by sex, age group and class (percentage)

Total Sample		Sex		Age Group			Class			
		Male	Female	15-17	18-20	21-24	A/B	C	D/E	NA
Yes	28.1	29.6	26.5	32.7	26.6	25.6	33.5	28.2	24.0	23.1
No	71.8	70.2	73.4	67.2	73.2	74.2	66.4	71.7	75.8	76.3
NA	0.1	0.2	0.1	0.1	0.2	0.2	0.1	0.1	0.2	0.6
Total	100	100	100	100	100	100	100	100	100	100

Source: Ibase/Pólis, *Pesquisa de Opinião Juventude Brasileira e Democracia: participação, esferas e políticas públicas*, 2005.

Level of schooling is a significant variable. Young people with more schooling participate more in groups: 30.5 per cent are in middle or higher education, 28.3 per cent have completed fundamental schooling, but not middle school, and 24.4 per cent have not finished fundamental schooling. The data demonstrate the significant influence of schooling on group-based youth activities.

Also, in addition to having their right to school denied, young people who are out of school miss important opportunities for civil training and for meeting other youth in shared public activities. The 28.1 per cent of the young people who reported participating in groups were asked what activity type was closest to their groups' aims. The activity types the groups relate to most significantly are religious (42.5 per cent), sports (32.5 per cent) and artistic – music, dance and theatre (26.9 per cent).

The activity types least mentioned were: student (11.7 per cent), communication (6.3 per cent), neighbourhood improvement (5.8 per cent), environment (4.5 per cent), political party

(4.3 per cent), volunteer work (1.3 per cent) and other activities (0.8 per cent). There is a clear predominance of religious activities in collective participation experiences. Studies of youth religiosity have pointed to the influence of friendship groups in their religious option. This important factor is configuring new situations of religious pluralism within families, characterized by the declining rates at which parents transfer their religion to their children (Novaes 2005).

Sports emerged as the second most significant group of activities, followed by those connected with artistic expression, confirming play and expression as prominent dimensions to any understanding of the interests that motivate young people in building their collective identities. Sports groups, in turn, are predominantly male – 46.2 per cent of men compared to 17.2 per cent of women. They reflect the socio-spatial division that is traditional in Brazil, where men have more mobility in society and the community. This is not just for practising sports, and applies to other times and places in the public sphere (Brenner, Carrano & Dayrell 2004).

Even though groups connected with artistic and cultural activities are not predominant, it is important to note that the most telling representations of contemporary youth are shaped around their individual and collective manifestations. Young people involved in these activities gain the most exposure in the public sphere, and they are the ones who search for or produce symbolic meanings, styles, collective identities and shared social attitudes. They adopt characteristic styles that mark their bodies and how they dress, consume and communicate, attracting the attention of the culture industries, which seek inspiration for producing 'young' goods that influence not only the younger generations, but all of consumer society. It is also youth culture groups, particularly music groups formed by young blacks, which have given visibility to the serious social problems experienced by residents in the peripheries of Brazil's major cities.

Gender does not affect the participation rates in artistic and cultural activities groups however, they are the most frequent option for participation by the young people with greatest purchasing power. Participation in this case is more frequent among the younger groups (32.3 per cent in the 15 to 17 year age group) than among the older groups (21.5 per cent in the 21 to 24 group). It is also more pronounced among those who did not complete fundamental schooling (34.0 per cent) than among those who completed middle school or more (22.1 per cent), confirming the constraints that come with advancing years.

Participation in social movements

'Have you ever participated in any movement or meeting to improve life in your neighbourhood or city?'. With that question we sought to learn about young people's involvement in collective action directed to improving conditions of life in their country.

Table 2 – Participation in movements to improve neighbourhood / city conditions (percentage)

Total Sample		Sex		Age Group			Class		
		Male	Female	15-17	18-20	21-24	A/B	C	D/E
Yes	18.5	19.0	17.9	14.8	18.4	21.3	16.9	17.2	22.0
No	80.6	80.0	81.2	84.2	80.9	77.6	81.1	82.2	77.7
NA	0.9	1.0	0.9	1.0	0.7	1.1	2.0	0.6	0.3
Total	100	100	100	100	100	100	100	100	100

Source: Ibase/Polis, *Pesquisa de Opinião Juventude Brasileira e Democracia: participação, esferas e políticas públicas*, 2004.

Of the respondents, 18.5 per cent reported having taken part, while 80.6 per cent said they have never been involved in any type of social movement or collective action in their neighbourhood or city. Unlike what happens with the groups where participants are mostly younger, community participation predominantly involves the older youth (21.3 per cent between 21 and 24 years old) rather than the younger respondents (14.8 per cent between 15 and 17 years old). It is also the poorer youth (classes D/E) who participate more (22.0 per cent) in movements for community improvements in comparison with 16.9 per cent of the wealthier youth (classes A/B).

The study asked the young people who did participate about the nature of their neighbourhood or city activities. The main goals were to gain or improve: leisure areas or sports facilities (37.8 per cent), education/school (36.5 per cent), safety (34.1 per cent), sanitation/environment (29.2 per cent) and clinics (27.2 per cent). When disaggregated, the data reveal significant differentiation by gender, age and social class.

Males, particularly between 15 and 17 years old and from classes A/B, mobilize primarily around goals connected with leisure and sports facilities (43.7 per cent men and 31.7 per cent women). The main reason for community mobilization by women, however, was safety, a concern for 36.8 per cent of the young women and 31.6 per cent of the young men who had engaged in this type of activity. Organization around safety is greater among the wealthier sector of youth (38.3 per cent) than among the poorer (31.8 per cent), with the latter being more motivated by issues connected with education/school (38.7 per cent). Those with most schooling were more involved on the issue of safety, even though the issues of leisure and sports facilities prompted significant involvement.

The study also asked about social and political engagement. It asked young people whether or not they participated in more institutionalized groups, organizations or movements at the time of the survey, and whether they had participated previously, but no longer did so. Current participation in religious institutions was again the highest reported by those interviewed (15.3 per cent). The next most common was involvement in sports/leisure clubs or associations (8.3 per cent) and artistic groups (5.5 per cent). Interestingly, in all areas of participation, those who had participated in the past were more numerous that those who are participating at present.

A loss of interest and trust in groups and organizations might explain why more young people participated in groups and organizations in the past than were participating at the time of the survey. However, the decline in involvement with institutions should not in itself be taken to indicate apathy towards social participation. Involvement in non-institutionalized causes, or in issues with more visible outcomes in the short term, or in more autonomously perceived actions compared with the classic spheres of political participation may be compensating for low levels of *institutional social capital* (Putnam 2002).

The datum that shows that more than 70 per cent of young people do not take part in any group or voluntary association should not lead us to qualify Brazilian youth as resistant to association-building. The significant number of young participants in religious, sports and cultural organizations and those who have become involved in movements to improve conditions in their neighbourhood or city must be considered. The lack of studies comparing participation among young people and adults precludes us from making value judgments on the possibility that young people may have deserted participation.

Perceptions on participation

When asked how they would classify their political participation in terms of three options, (i) 8.5 per cent of the young people considered themselves politically involved; (ii) another

65.6 per cent said they tried to keep themselves informed, but without participating personally; and (iii) 24.7 per cent declared they made no effort to inform themselves about politics nor did they participate personally. Those over the age of 18 (18.9 per cent) and those with most schooling (10.2 per cent) – who had completed middle school or more – were the ones who considered themselves most politically involved. The youngest (15-17 years old) and those who had not completed fundamental schooling (38.3 per cent) were the ones most likely to say they did not try to inform themselves nor participate personally in political matters.

It is revealing that most of the young people interviewed showed interest in political issues, thus rejecting the *politically alienated* stigma. This is a designation commonly found in the media, which ingenuously and anachronistically compare young people today with militants of the past. Although they do not participate directly in spaces recognized as being of the political domain, they do participate in a certain sphere of politics by seeking information on political activities.

The last question asked in the opinion survey was whether they were interested, and available to take part, in meetings with other young people to dialogue on subjects relating to Brazilian youth, to which 57 per cent of the interviewees responded affirmatively. More young women (59.7 per cent) than young men (54.2 per cent) were interested and showed a willingness to take part. Age also proved an important factor: young people between 15 and 17 years old were most willing (60.2 per cent), compared to those between 21 and 24 years old (52.6 per cent). Once again this underlines that the young adults are less available or willing to engage in participatory activities.

The young people surveyed did not reject politics outright. However, they did send messages that reflect a profound mistrust of the traditional operators of politics – 'politicians' in the broadest sense. In this study, the data do not portray a rejection of political participation, but they do indicate a lack of confidence in the institutional channels, in the traditional ways of doing politics and in their party operators. At the same time as there is little confidence in anything resembling traditional politics, the emergence of other spheres of participation that need to be better understood by social researchers is perceived. Some youth groups lend new meanings to politics and – drawing on other logics and sensibilities – develop multiple forms and content for collective action in the public sphere. Research has to be broadened so as to extend our understanding of the ways that these young people participate in building new public spheres and can contribute to redefining the meanings of politics.

It is important to remember that 28.1 per cent of the young people reported forming part of some kind of group. This is the basic, voluntary public sphere, the existence of which expresses a certain potential for association and participation. Groups directed at religious, sporting and artistic purposes represent the substrate of youth association-building in Brazil today and constitute a significant youth civil society arranging collective actions. These groups are not always acknowledged as politically or socially significant, but do exist as collective subjects building *cultural citizenship* (Cruz 2003).[3]

Cefaï (2007: 92) states that in France too, young people have shown a loss of confidence in the classic institutions of political participation, such as parties and trade unions, and have preferred to place their political commitment in less formal associations. The 'crisis of representation' is also reflected in the high rates of electoral abstention among the 18 to 25 year olds. Thus,

> (…) political commitment among the 18 to 25 year olds no longer occurs in party or trade union organizations, but in associations. Mobilization is concentrated more in small, local structures – and one can see the attraction exerted over the young by small, everyday causes

that are closer, more concrete and more controllable – although it also goes hand in hand with phenomena of adhesion to international organizations such as Greenpeace. Countless associations in favour of the unemployed, homeless and undocumented immigrants, and against racism and the National Front, have also come together to form a galaxy of associative networks that combine, at the same time, very concrete goals and important moral aims and exert a strong attraction on the younger. Nor should we forget the commitment of Catholics and Muslims.

The proper distinctions must be maintained between the situations in France and Brazil – especially the particular situation of immigrants and the generation of French Arabs who have not been incorporated as full citizens. However, there are similarities regarding the declining popularity of political parties and trade unions and adhesion to causes relating to the 'small, everyday causes' that can be more readily understood and controlled by young participants.

The feelings that contribute to the formation of youth collectivities are directed mainly to the planes of sociability, shared cultural activities and collective subjectivity. Groups set their own rules for deliberation and contribute to their young participants' forming opinions of their own. Groups are important in that they allow young people to exercise autonomy of thought and action that they often cannot exercise in the presence of adults. This is especially true when the latter defines the 'rules of play' of institutional power. The spheres of youth association-building can be places for formulating and creating, for forming thoughtful publics and addressing problems, which may or may not lead to public policies. The latter depends on the ability of collective actors to influence the policy agenda.

It is in that respect that groups can be considered laboratories for democratic public affairs and their practices must be experienced in the spaces where diverse individuals meet in the cities. Public policies in this regard can favour encounters among the various youth groups, so that they can recognize each other in democratic, participatory public settings. It is therefore useful to distinguish between the public sociability that exists within youth groups – which in themselves are not democratic spaces – from the broader public spheres characterized by multiple forms of solidarity, collective action and democratically mediated conflicts. Opportunities must also be created for those young people whose sociability is simple and unconnected from membership of any group. This could definitely be a task for democracies to perform when updating school agendas.

Final remarks

Young people's responses about their main group activities indicate that their motivations to act collectively in the public sphere are directed mostly to practical ends around everyday life values. The question thus arises of how to arouse interest in national or global issues, spaces and problems that may seem worlds away to young people whose sense of participation is directed towards what is close at hand and everyday.

How can horizons of time and place be broadened for young people physically and symbolically imprisoned in poor neighbourhoods that suffer violence from drug traffickers and the police forces and lack even the minimum urban infrastructure necessary for plural social, cultural and collective living? Young people's concerns about violence in the cities are an issue that deserves proper attention from policy makers. History has already shown that liberties may be sacrificed in trying to ensure security, unless democratic institutional channels are set up to solve the problems that beset individuals and collectivities.

The figures of this survey express the encouraging fact that most of the young people interviewed demonstrate interest in political matters. This means that, even though many of them do not participate directly in spaces known recognized as political domain, they do participate in a specific public sphere by seeking information on the subject. The study provides clues to understanding the social and political processes that orient these young people's ideas and practices.

Interestingly, considering the overall study data, young people denounce factors that hinder them from exercising their citizenship fully. While at the same time, young people give suggestions for policies – especially in education, culture, and job and income generation – to favour building youth citizenship on autonomous, democratic bases.

The survey has brought to light difficulties that need to be surmounted in Brazil if youth participation is to be broadened in a society that deprives large parts of its youth the basic rights of citizenship. Public policies to stimulate youth participation cannot be indifferent to the impediments facing young people, especially the poorer ones, which prevent them from making a livelihood and planning their lives. Policy must therefore take account of the scarcity of opportunities for training, participation and social integration. Democratic policies need to start with realistic diagnoses of the objective conditions young people can build on in order to set themselves up as social stakeholders who participate in public life.

Recognition of the impediments to participation will then become an important factor in overcoming these problems. The challenge is to formulate public policies to mobilize resources and social involvement in order to allow young people to make alternative choices and establish themselves as subjects of their own lives. Emancipatory policies that foster participation are those able to remove the obstacles that prevent personal and collective projects from taking shape, block channels of participation and foreclose places and times where dialogue, cooperation and conflict are practiced in the public sphere.

References

Cefaï, Daniel, *Acción asociativa y ciudadanía común: La sociedad civil como matriz de la res publica?* INJUV/ES. Available at: <http://www.injuve.mtas.es/injuve/contenidos.downloadatt.action?id=1395427125>. Accessed on: 15 Apr. 2007.

Cruz, Rossana Reguillo, *Emergencia de culturas juveniles: Estrategias del desencanto*, Grupo Editorial Norma (Bogotá, 2000).

Ibase/Pólis, *Juventude Brasileira e Democracia: participação, esferas e políticas públicas*, Final research report, Ibase/Pólis (Rio de Janeiro, 2005).

Krauskopf, Dina, 'Desafíos en la construcción y implementación de las políticas de juventud en América Latina', in *El futuro ya no es como antes: ser joven en América Latina. Revista Nueva Sociedad*, Nov-Dec 2005, pp. 141-153, (Buenos Aires, 2005).

León, Oscar Dávila, 'La década perdida en política de juventud en Chile; o la década del aprendizaje doloroso?', in León, O. D. (Ed.) *Políticas públicas de juventud en América Latina: políticas nacionales*, pp. 129-166, Cidpa (Chile, 2003).

Margulis, Mario & Urresti, Marcelo, 'La juventud es más que una palabra', in Margulis, M. (Ed.) *La juventud es más que una palabra*, pp. 13-31, Biblos (Buenos Aires, 1996).

Melucci, Alberto, *O jogo do eu: a mudança de si em uma sociedade global*, Unisinos (São Leopoldo/RS, 2004).

Novaes, Regina, 'Juventude, percepções e comportamentos: a religião faz diferença?', in *Retratos da Juventude Brasileira: análises de uma pesquisa nacional*, Helena Wendel Abramo & Pedro Paulo Martoni Branco (Eds.), pp. 263-290, Instituto Cidadania/Fundação Perseu Abramo (São Paulo, 2005).

Putnam, Robert D., *Comunidade e Democracia: a experiência da Itália Moderna*, FGV (Rio de Janeiro, 2002).

Reguillo, Rossana, 'Ciudadanías juveniles en América Latina', *Última Década* xx/19 (2003), pp. 11-30, CIDPA (Chile, 2003).

Santos, Milton, *Técnica, espaço, tempo: globalização e meio técnico-científico informacional*, Hucitec (São Paulo, 1994).

Sposito, M. & Carrano, P., 'Juventude e políticas públicas no Brasil', *Revista Brasileira de Educação* xxiv (2003), pp. 16-39, Autores Associados (São Paulo, 2003).

Chapter 2

SCHOOL AND YOUTH PARTICIPATION
(Re)thinking the Links

*Juarez Tarcísio Dayrell**
Geraldo Pereira Magela Leão
Nilma Lino Gomes

In recent years, discussion of young people' social participation has nearly always turned fatalistic. Society perceives the lack of socio-political participation by young people and hastily holds them responsible, generally comparing them

---

* About the authors:
Juarez Tarcísio Dayrell is responsible for the study in the Belo Horizonte metropolitan region. He is Associate Professor at the Education Faculty (FAE), Minas Gerais Federal University (UFMG), Ph.D. in Education (São Paulo University, USP) and coordinator of the FAE/UFMG Youth Observatory (*Observatório da Juventude*).
Geraldo Pereira Magela Leão is responsible for the study in the Belo Horizonte metropolitan region, Associate Professor at the Education Faculty (FAE/UFMG), Ph.D. in Education (USP) and member of the coordination of the FAE/UFMG Youth Observatory.
Nilma Lino Gomes is responsible for the study in the Belo Horizonte metropolitan region, Associate Professor at the Education Faculty (FAE/UFMG), Ph.D. in Social Anthropology (USP), member of the coordination of the FAE/UFMG Youth Observatory and coordinator of the UFMG's Affirmative Action Programme.

with other, supposedly 'more participatory' generations. Besides reinforcing stereotypes of 'alienated youth', this view leads to a prescriptive approach holding onto an ideal of youth participation that fails to match young people's expectations or the conditions necessary for them to engage in social and political action.

More than calling attention to youth participation or the lack of it, what is needed is to question the context in which young people are seeking, in one way or another, a place in society. What are their social and economic circumstances and what role do these play in young Brazilians' participation experiences? What conditions and spaces are available for them to participate socially and politically? Does a young person's experience stimulate them to participate in such a context? It is fundamental that we examine the socio-economic and educational context influencing – or failing to influence – movement towards participation, and learn more about the places, times and situations young people find themselves in socially. This entails getting to know this generation of youth better, and considering the conditions they work under and their access to education and cultural goods. In addition, the questions and issues that most motivate them, and the spaces and frameworks that they inhabit must be studied.

In an attempt to explore the role that the educational experience is playing in the process in greater depth, we elaborate on some thinking about youth participation in the Belo Horizonte metropolitan region (BHMR). We ask ourselves how much the school organization model and its dynamics produce a favourable environment where youth participation can develop. This thinking is based on local and national data from the study *Brazilian Youth and Democracy: Participation, Spheres and Public Policies* (Ibase 2006), both its quantitative version (an opinion poll) and its qualitative version (the Dialogue Groups), which were conducted between July 2004 and November 2005.[1]

The socio-cultural profile of youth in the Belo Horizonte metropolitan region

The 'youth condition'

To begin with, one must recognize the difficulties in even defining 'youth' as a category: what is youth after all? This debate[2] has figured in the sociology of youth since its origins in the early 20th century and has been considered from the widest possible range of approaches. Stated briefly, the difficulties in defining a youth category can be said to stem in part from the fact that it constitutes a social condition and, at the same time, a type of representation (Peralva 1997).

Youth is understood here as a socially-constructed category that gains specific shapes in different historical, social and cultural contexts and is characterized by a diversity in conditions which include social (class origins, for instance), cultural (ethnicity, religious identity, values etc.), gender and even geographic, among others. Besides being shaped by its diversity, youth is a dynamic category that shifts as social changes take place in the course of history. In fact, rather than 'youth', what exists are young people, the individuals who experience and feel youth according to their specific socio-cultural context.

Rather than conceptualizing youth, we opted to work with the notion of 'youth condition' which we considered more appropriate to the aims of the discussion. From the Latin *conditio*, it refers to a mode of being, a situation in life, and in society. However, it also refers to the circumstances by which such a mode or situation can be ascertained. To speak of a 'youth condition' is therefore to speak in two dimensions. It refers to the way a society constitutes and gives meaning to that moment in the life cycle, in a historical and generational context. However, it also refers to a situation, that is, the way the condition is lived out in terms of the various aspects of social differentiation – class, gender, ethnicity, etc. Our analysis takes into account both the symbolic dimension and the factual, material, historical and political circumstances in which youth is socially produced (Abramo 2005; Margulis 2000).

Even when working with data that aggregate youth in the 15-24 age bracket, the various objective conditions and the perceptions of the senses of being young must be considered. We know that 'arbitrary aggregation by age does not summarize the identifications possible in a given set of men and women brought together in a research population, but it does make it possible to perceive common generational experiences' (Ibase 2006: 8). It therefore allows us to think about a portion of the population that have the same times and places in common when speaking of sensibilities, knowledges, memories, and historical and cultural experiences.

In this way, we think about aspects of the youth condition of BHMR residents, with a view to exploring our understanding of who these young people are in greater depth, followed by an analysis of their experiences of social participation. Finally, we will discuss the role of school and school experiences in this process.

The youth condition's multiple dimensions in the BHMR

A first aspect of the youth condition is the family relationship. Data from the opinion poll[3] indicate that the large majority of the interviewees (89.2 per cent) are single, suggesting that they still live with their family of origin. However, a significant percentage (9.5 per cent) of the young people are married or living together. These figures underline the trend towards postponing the moment of independence from the family, which is reiterated by other studies on the prolongation of youth.

Consistent with these figures, the great majority (81.8 per cent) have no children. However, nearly twice as many youth have children (18 per cent) than are married. This is evidence that a good number of young people are parents, but do not live together, which is common in cases of teenage pregnancy, for instance. Even though the figures do not permit more substantial inferences, some studies consider active sexuality dissociated from the reproductive function to be a feature of the contemporary youth condition (Abramo 2005). This situation provides the grounds for examining gender relations and what part these play in shaping the youth condition in Brazil.

Another dimension that affects the youth condition is colour/race. In this study, a large number of the interviewees (36.5 per cent) classified themselves as 'brown', while 19.3 per cent classified themselves as 'black'. Adding these two figures together we can see that the 'black race' totals 55.8 per cent of the population. The significant difference between the percentages of brown and black is interesting and may signal difficulty in accepting a black identity, a phenomenon observed in other studies. Finally, 35.1 per cent of the young people considered themselves 'white', 5.3 per cent 'yellow' and 3.1 per cent 'indigenous'.

Religion is also a constituent of the youth condition and, as will be seen below, occupies an important place among the loci of youth participation. In this study, most of the young people interviewed in the BHMR declared themselves to be Catholic (61.5 per cent), followed by Evangelical/Protestant (22.7 per cent). A smaller percentage are Spiritualist (1.8 per cent); followers of Eastern religions (0.3 per cent); Jewish (0.1 per cent) and followers of Afro-Brazilian religions (0.1 per cent). It is important to note that a significant percentage of young people (9.5 per cent) declared that they believe in God, but do not belong to any religion. Only 1.6 per cent responded that they do not believe in God.

Young people and work

Unlike in European countries, youth in the BHMR and in Brazil in general, do not characteristically benefit from any moratorium on working. The study indicated that, in the BHMR, 41.7 per cent of the young people between 15 and 24 years of age were working. For this contingent, work is a factor that enables them to experience the youth condition by assuring them the necessary minimum resources for leisure, courting or consumption. Most of the group (37.9 per cent) were formally employed, while 20.1 per cent were working without having signed labour documents and 22.3 per cent declared themselves self-employed.

Studies indicate that it is common to start working at a variety of 'odd jobs' during adolescence, with this instability tending to persist throughout youth. This study confirms that finding, since when the two latter percentages are summed, 42.4 per cent of the young people can be considered to be in a precarious work situation, with no proof of experience nor any qualification with which to improve their placement in the market.

Correlating these data with social class, schooling and colour makes clear the perverse effect of social inequality in the region and in Brazil. Poorer, black youth with less schooling – exactly those who require greater attention from the government – are the ones who work under the most precarious conditions.

Although gender was not taken into account as a focus in the study, including this category to these factors would possibly yield an even more complex picture of the relationship between youth and work. What we can say is that, for a large portion of the young people in the BHMR, the work world is a social setting that both includes and subordinates them.

Regarding the realities of youth unemployment, the study observed what other Brazilian studies have been reporting since the 1990s: unemployment rates are higher among youth than in any other age bracket. In the sample surveyed, 58.3 per cent of the young people were not working. Most (64.5 per cent) of these were looking for work at the time of the study, which may reveal the difficulties young people face when looking for their first job, a phenomenon still awaiting solutions from government.

It is no surprise that the issue of work came up as one of the young people's major concerns during the Dialogue Groups. The discussions emphasized the need to expand the labour market, reinforcing how central the 'first job' issue is. Another major concern voiced in the groups is how unemployment is associated with a lack of opportunities to learn a profession through internships or vocational courses. Furthermore young people communicated a demand that deserves special attention - an end to prejudice, particularly with regards to race and gender. 'If it's between a blonde girl and a mulatta, you can be sure – and this happened in my neighbourhood – they'll give preference to the blonde'.

In short, for a large portion of young people, the work world could be considered as a mediator, both actually and symbolically, in how they experience the youth condition. Along with other social dimensions, work can be said to 'make youths', even when the diversity of young people's situations and attitudes with regard to it are considered.

Sociability, culture and leisure

Another dimension of the youth condition is sociability. The centrality of this issue is made clear in a series of studies[4] on the subject. Sociability develops in peer groups, especially at places and during times of leisure and entertainment, but also in institutional settings such as school and work. Sociability appears to respond to young people's need for communication, solidarity, democracy, autonomy, exchange of emotionality and, particularly, identity.

In this study, sociability emerges as a dimension underlying two others: access to culture and leisure, and social participation in groups. In the Dialogue Groups, the young people discussed culture and leisure and raised some important issues. The first relates to access itself since they refer to work as a precondition for leisure activities, demonstrating that increasingly leisure is determined by market relations anchored in the consumer capacity of young people and their families (Brenner 2005). What the young people make clear is that, more and more, any cultural or leisure activity entails costs such as travel fares and admission prices.

This situation clearly reflects the restricted range of leisure options open to a large portion of Brazil's youth population, allied with how ineffectual the democratization of culture has been in Brazil, as noted in other studies.[5] The demands made in the Dialogue Groups were consistent with these realities as young people demanded that cultural and leisure facilities be decentralized and better distributed across the metropolitan region in order to ensure free public access.

Under these circumstances, school emerges as a demand in terms of culture/leisure. It resurfaces as one of the only public facilities and places available to poor communities. This justifies the demands for schools to be opened on weekends or for culture centres to be built at schools. In addition to access, the need for cultural events to be better publicized was also raised. They argued that although there are free, public cultural events in the city, the information does not reach all young people. This information is restricted to the central regions and the middle strata of the population.

It is also important to note is that shopping centers feature prominently as leisure settings. These can be regarded as an alternative, given the lack of public meeting places, but also as 'safe' places, underlining the relationship between leisure and violence. During the Dialogue Groups, the issue of violence emerged several times as one of the young people's greatest concerns.

Given the modern-day plague of banal violence, young people's demand for safety in peripheral areas, is the same as the concern among urban, middle-class adults. Feelings of insecurity in Brazil are a fact of life. However, we know that the sum total of social, racial and gender inequalities plus extreme poverty, leads to a tendency to stereotype poor, young, black males from peripheral communities as more violent. As such they are the main victims of police violence. These young people suffer from a terrible dilemma since they live at the crossroads of social, racial, gender and police violence. In that context, just like any citizen, they claim the freedom to come and go in safety and demand that the police ethically perform their duty.

Social participation in youth groups is another dimension that organizes young people's sociability, culture and leisure. This participation will be examined later, but here it is important to raise some points directly related with the youth condition. Although the survey shows a relatively small number of young people involved in cultural groups, we should not disregard a trend detected in other studies. Culture appears to be the preferred dimension for the practices, representations, symbols and rituals young people use to demarcate a youth identity. That is to say that, in the existing context of diversity, the youth condition is experienced through symbolic mediation reflected in the widest variety of cultural expressions. For this reason, cultural groups take on a significant role. They make possible the practices, relationships and symbols through which young people set up their own spaces, expanding the circuits and networks where exchange takes place and which are the preferred means by which they enter the public sphere.

Access to information

Asked where they usually obtain their information, the large majority of the young people from the BHMR said television (83 per cent), followed by newspapers and magazines (52.7 per cent), radio (49.2 per cent), friends, group or colleagues at work (24.3 per cent), Internet (21.5 per cent), family (17.8 per cent) and, lastly, teachers (13.3 per cent) and school friends (11.8 per cent). Interestingly, school has ceased to be the prime source of information for new generations, reinforcing the need to rethink its social function. At the same time, the results demonstrate the centrality of the media. This cultural trait which is characteristic of contemporary youth cultures calls for further research.

Access to the digital media – The computer and the Internet deserve more detailed analysis because of their importance in how information is accessed and distributed. In the Belo Horizonte metropolitan region, only 42.2 per cent of young people reported having access to a computer. Significant differences emerge in terms of social categories, such as social class, race/colour, schooling or school type. Therefore the profile of most young people with access is white, upper- and middle-class with higher education after private schooling. Even fewer had Internet access: 34.5 per cent of the young people reported accessing the Internet, just over one third of the young people in the BHMR. There were no significant differences by gender or age, but once again socio-economic characteristics proved a major turning point by replicating the same situation as described above.

The data provide evidence that digital inclusion is intimately linked to people's ability to purchase computers in a context where micro-credit policies are scarce. They also show that public digital networks are not extensive and have little capillary penetration. This indicates that measures taken towards digital democracy have not reached most of the BHMR young people and that access to digital media and the Internet continues to favour the elite. There is therefore a demand for government action to promote not just access, but also digital literacy, both of which are just as important today as access to and mastery of reading and writing.

Social participation and youth policy

The figures show that 20.7 per cent of young people in the BHMR participate in some kind of group of some kind which coincides with other studies on the subject. Generally speaking, that percentage yields different levels of participation according to personal attributes (gender, age), schooling and social background.[6] Participation appears to be increasing among younger middle- and upper-class young people with more schooling.

Of the young people who took part in a group of some kind, 43.5 per cent engaged in religious activities and 27.1 per cent in cultural activities (such as music, dance and theatre). The groups that pursued sports activities accounted for 26.6 per cent. In the remaining types of activities, the percentages fall off significantly. This highlights the relative insignificance of the classic settings for participation, such as political parties and even student movements, which was mentioned by only 3.4 per cent of the young people.

In addition to religion and sport, leisure and culture activities very clearly have a strong presence, together involving more than half of the young people. This points to the motivating power of activities here symbolic meanings and collective identities are produced, whether these are specific cultural styles or shared social attitudes. This fact has already been signalled in other studies. (Sposito 2000; Melucci 1997).

Although cited by a less significant number (7.7 per cent) of respondents, participation in community movements raises some important issues to address. In this case participation tendencies are greater among the poorer, black and older young people. Although few young people presently participate, when asked if they had participated in any movement or meeting to improve life in their neighbourhood or city in the past, the percentage rose to 19.9 per cent. One hypothesis which remains to be investigated is whether young people possibly join in concrete action that yields short term results towards some kind of improvement in their neighbourhood or residence and does not require ongoing daily involvement.

Perceptions of participation

In the quantitative stage of the study, the young people were presented with phrases and asked to position themselves with regard to each of them, in an effort to gauge their perceptions of participation and politics.[7] The respondents seemed divided between adhering to and valuing collective causes and supporting individualistic solutions. Generally, they tended to reproduce the commonly held negative images of politicians and their activities, revealing a remote and prejudiced view of the world of traditional politics.

These perceptions became evident in the Dialogue Groups, where the young people tended to reject any possibility of engaging in traditional forms of political participation, such as political parties, trade unions, the student movement or other social movements. While recognizing that these channels are important to satisfying social demands, they seemed to regard that kind of participation as institutional government action, and not as action by young people in frameworks like the student movement, student unions, etc. Our hypothesis is that a lack of knowledge about 'political activities', and engagement in collective pursuits, may be one of the reasons for this restricted view.

It also appears that the young people are indicating that more organized political participation belongs to the adult world. Moreover, they reduce political participation to the airing of grievances to established institutions such as the city council, city councillors or municipal government, which is a very specific form of traditional political engagement. We can infer that, generally speaking, the young people do not see themselves as stakeholders or agents that can intervene in their reality and in institutions. This appears to demonstrate a certain disbelief in the more traditional forms of political engagement, a lack of any broad knowledge of political affairs and little experience in action of this kind. However, it also is an alert that young people view limited scope for intervening in their own reality as stakeholders, subjects and citizens.

Young people's selection of volunteer work as their ideal form of political activity demonstrates the tension between a favourable view of collective action and disbelief in the effectiveness of collective social and political action. The young people regarded – nearly always collective – volunteer action as the path by which it was possible for them to achieve their demands. It was clear in the discussions that they are aware of the limitations of this kind of participatory involvement, but admit that 'at least it is something'. Their arguments suggested that this was the most flexible path in terms of available time and the degree of involvement demanded, and permitted different levels of engagement. The fact that this kind of action produces immediate, visible results, in addition to permitting direct control was an additional attractive aspect.

A number of hypotheses arise to explain young people's perceptions of participation in public life. The emphasis on volunteer work may reflect the lack of channels for participation, which makes it impossible to stimulate, far less to experiment with, differentiated forms of social participation and also leads to disbelief in the effectiveness of collective action. It may also express the tension between solidarity and the Brazilian experience in this historical context, which is marred by social inequalities. In this situation, solidarity tends to follow a welfare work pattern, which is present in all social strata and reinforced by institutional religious practices. In this way, volunteer action as a cultural expression, is naturalized as a consequence of young people's 'good intentions'.

These data warrant an effort to produce denser theory on the subject to help. This could help us understand how young people position themselves in relation to national realities and the approaches move towards to actively engage in the social and political life of the country. We feel it is just as important to reflect on the role of school in this context, given that it is one of the few public institutions that more or less universally affects Brazilian youth. What relationship can we establish between youth participation and public school? What are the limits and scope of this institution regarding the social condition of Brazilian youth?

Youth participation: some thoughts

As mentioned above, we are trying to avoid reaching pessimistic conclusions and to go beyond the idealizations surrounding youth participation in the past. While the percentages preclude making comparisons with past generations, similarly there is little data on socio-political participation by the general population. This makes it difficult to know whether youth is the only segment that does not show high rates of participation or whether this is the case for the entire population.

One hypothesis that could explain the low rates of social and political participation by young people in the BHMR is the socio-economic context most of them live in, which does not encourage the hope and belief that their collective action may be capable of affecting their realities in any way. Nor does the context offer the means for creating habits and values favourable to exercise and learn about participation. This leads us to conclude that it is rather difficult to make democracy effective without a minimum level of equality in life conditions. The lack of spaces and situations for exercising and learning collective affairs and social participation must also be considered, since it is this kind of experimentation that allows young people to believe that acting collectively can bring results.

Another important aspect to address is the time and pace of contemporary youth, as indicated above. Studies show that youth participation has been characteristically fluid, nomadic and intermittent and also point to one-off group arrangements with goals that are specific and in the present.

These features are connected with the broad changes that have come about in complex societies, such as the speed of technological change, which heightens the uncertainties characteristic of our day and age (Leccardi 1991). Therefore, it is possible to argue that the spaces and stimuli for exercising and learning participation, as well as the relationship young people have with time, are variables that affect whether they effectively become involved in social and political matters.

One final thought has to do with the type of group and activity that young people are involved with. It is possible to raise the hypothesis, already voiced in other papers and discussions, that a participation process is underway which is distancing itself from the settings of formal politics, but is gaining strength in other types of collective actions in the public sphere. The data in this study indicate that the classical political arrangements, such as political parties and trade unions and even the student movement, are losing ground as the preferred settings for youth participation. Young people seem to be rejecting these traditional forms of participation, particularly where they are dominated by the vices of patronage and nepotism.

This phenomenon is also observed in other countries. In Europe, for example, studies indicate that young people are distancing themselves from trade unions, but not rejecting them; they mistrust political parties, but acknowledge a diffuse interest without the corresponding participation; and they seek politics without traditional labels designating left- or right-wing positions (Sposito 2000; Bendit 2000).

At the same time, young people show themselves to be more involved not just with religious activities, but with leisure and cultural groups and associations. This may indicate a broadening of collective youth interests and practices that produce coalescence around social interaction, collective practices and common interests. This kind of involvement points to youth identity and the very right to live one's youth as possible motivations for social participation.

In addition, new forms of action and new issues seem to be connected to collective actions that take place in multiple forms and with varying degrees of social intervention in fluid rather than structured manners.

In light of the social condition of Brazilian youth, their participation experiences and their perceptions of politics, we must also question the role of schools, particularly public schools. To what extent does the institution of school foster experiences that stimulate learning and experimentation in social and political participation? Have the form and content of school organization prioritized schooling that enables young people to critically position themselves and envisage forms of collective action around their demands? Is it concerned with stimulating their participation in how schools are run and autonomous student organizations? From the point of view of social and political participation, what place does school occupy in young people's lives?

School and youth participation

School has a place in young people's lives. The question is what place that is and how it relates to youth participation.

The figures show that school is not absent from the lives of these young people, especially those from classes D and E. However, only 32.4 per cent have completed middle school, while 45.8 per cent did not finish middle school and 21.8 per cent only finished fundamental schooling. It is important to note that 54.5 per cent of the young people surveyed were not studying at the time of the survey, which indicates that we are still a long way from guaranteeing universal access to education.

In addition to the visible inequality in access to education, we should ask ourselves: what kind of school do young people attend, even if irregularly? Is it organizing itself to serve these individuals in their condition as young people? Serving them entails not just universalizing education, but assuring the physical, educational and symbolic conditions these and other individuals need at this time of their life. It also means building school facilities capable of leveraging the social networks that are characteristic of our human condition and so very present in the context of the youth condition.

One option would be to promote collective activities that stimulate participation in the school, such as debates, films and visits to exhibitions that enhance the quality of the young people's education. Other appropriate activities could be characterized as social activities, such as excursions and parties; solidarity-based activities, such as community action or social work; and cultural activities, such as theatre, dance, music or cultural festivals.

The quantitative study showed that fewer than 50 per cent of the schools, both public and private, offer the kinds of activities mentioned above. Community action or social work activities constituted only a minor presence, and there were no significant differences in terms of social-class background, level of schooling or type of school. Therefore it is possible to infer that school has not stimulated its students, nor has it been a place for collective solidarity activities.

Only 33.6 per cent of the young people interviewed reported cultural activities at the schools they attend. Practically two thirds of schools in the BHMR did not stimulate or organize cultural activities in 2004, which proves how far removed they are from the world of young people. If cultural activities form part of the way young people live their lives, shouldn't the school that serves this public include such activities in its timetable and on its premises?

In addition to this low percentage, it is also striking that cultural activities (festive events and so on) are more common at the schools attended by young people in classes D/E (35.8 per cent) than classes A/B (30.7 per cent), and more so at public schools (34.7 per cent) than at private schools (26.6 per cent). Additionally, these activities are more present in fundamental schooling (35.4 per cent) and middle school (36.3 per cent) than in higher education (23.7 per cent).

Certain inferences can be made about the possible forms of participation described above. The lack of public leisure and culture facilities in poor communities may explain why schools attended by young people from classes D/E hold more cultural activities that those attended by classes A/B. In these cases, school becomes one of the few public places where poor youth can engage in such activities.

The figure above seems to indicate that, despite adverse conditions, public schools can still be a place where collective activities are held for poor youth, permitting them some level of youth participation. The issues that then arise are: How are these activities organized? Who are the young people who take part? Do these schools manage to dialogue with the world of youth culture production in their surrounding neighbourhoods and to interconnect it with young people's experience of school?

Another inference has to do with the decline in such activities at higher levels of schooling. Schools are less likely to have cultural or leisure facilities or a place where collective action is possible since they are more fixed in the world of 'thinking' and less in the world of 'doing' usually attributed to the adult world. However, this tendency may change with regards to public and private universities, perhaps giving grounds for another type of interpretation.

Also, the fact that culture, leisure and festive activities are found in schools, especially those with students from classes C, D and E, does not tell us anything about their quality. Often such activities are used as a way of occupying time at school and do not actually contribute to broadening – particularly poor – young people's cultural capital. It seems to us that these schools tend to exploit relationships for the purpose of discipline and habit-formation, to the detriment of bringing greater quality to human relations.

Meanwhile, the opposite trend is observed in informational activities. The survey shows that films, debates, seminars, visits to museums and exhibitions are more present in schools attended by classes A/B. Similarly, these activities were proportionately more present at higher education private schools than at public or middle schools. These figures seem to show the tendency for private schools to favour academic activities over cultural or social activities.

The figures reveal that at most of the schools attended by these young people, particularly the poorer ones, activities that may be considered basic to any quality educational process are either carried out inadequately or not at all. This calls into question the orientation of the educational work done at these institutions, which appears to be directed more towards intramural school activities than to any interaction with the outside world. Additionally, one may question whether the physical conditions and technological equipment exist which would permit videos to be shown or Internet work to be carried out, for example.

It is also important to discuss whether or not debates are held in schools. We know that when these activities are properly organized they can become a valuable channel for information and a place to learn how to argue, discuss, exchange opinions and so on. The public and private schools attended by the BHMR young people organized debating activities of different profiles and through programs of varying intensities. The results of the study indicate that these activities were not central to these schools' educational purposes. When they did take place they addressed the following topics: electoral politics, AIDS, sexuality, drugs, violence, human rights, the [school's] political and educational project, rules, discipline and forms of evaluation in school and, lastly, urban issues, such as problems in the neighbourhood and the city.

Data analysis suggests that the schools are not very open to holding activities that go beyond the transmission of formal subject-matter. When they do, their provision is inadequate and precarious. Few teaching institutions create participatory situations favourable to solidarity or strengthening sociability, or which provide access to cultural activities and knowledge.

In the context of the youth condition, being poor and a student at a public school permits other ways of experiencing and expressing that condition as compared with being young at a middle-class, private school. The inclusion of the gender and race dimensions may provide another picture of the youth condition, as well as the relationships among youth, school and youth participation.

The role of schools in young people's concerns and demands

Simply because youth turn their attention to school in order to question it, not necessarily to affirm the importance of its in the course of their youth, does not mean that this institution is not one of their concerns. The Dialogue Groups made it clear that although school consumes a large part of young people's time, school education ranks fourth among concerns, being mentioned by only 14 per cent of the young people. Higher education and access to it were cited by only a small number of young people during the Dialogue Groups, despite the surveys finding high rates of exclusion from tertiary education.

The young people voice concrete demands in relation to school. They demand better-qualified teachers in order to develop a closer human and educational relationship with students. This demand overshadows the recognition that more funding is needed for education.

A striking feature of the five Dialogue Groups was the feeling of indignation and disappointment in relation to school. The young people complained of a type of human and educational relationship based on disrespect and scorn for the people being educated, and demanded a different posture from school and from teachers. This would seem to indicate a cultural and generational clash between students and teachers and disrespect for students as social subjects and citizens with rights.

Some young people went as far as to say that 'the young teachers are the worst. They don't listen to us, they say that now they've graduated and it's our hard luck'. It is important to note that rather than the material and physical conditions of schools, young people call into doubt the human relationships developed at school. This situation deserves further thought, since educational times, spaces, curricula and projects are accomplished with real people. So if the educational relationship, as a human and professional relationship, is going badly, how is school supposed to rouse young people's interest in greater participation? How can it make use of the possible options for reorganizing school time and space? How will it be able to involve young people in work projects? How will it stimulate them to participate in the various democratic processes within the school?

'Extra-curricular' activities: school at the weekends

According to local and national data, the number of young people who frequent schools on the weekends varies. Only 14.2 per cent of the young people in the BHMR frequent schools or universities on weekends. Hypotheses for this low level of participation may be that the schools and universities do not open on the weekends or that young people are uninformed about what the school is used for at these times or they are simply uninterested in taking part. These inferences can be substantiated only by in-depth research on socio-economic, ethnicity/race and gender attributes aspects.

The figures do signal some ways forward to strengthen the relationship between school, young people and youth participation. Out-of-class activities, when properly structured and conceived as a student's right as well as the right of their family, can result in a different kind of organization for schools, particularly public schools. Through these activities, schools are better administered as a time and place and their relationship with the community improves.

Neighbouring NGOs, social movements, youth culture groups and so on, can be partners in this endeavour. It is not a question of social and government projects to open schools on the weekend. Over and beyond these measures, which are not contemplated at all schools, there is the possibility for specific capacity-building projects with cultural agents, who in their free time can interrelate school subject-matter with a variety of cultural approaches.

Final remarks

Although participation is still timid when compared to the potential for youth action, this study shows the paths, possibilities and problems that young people encounter to participate in society. One possible reason for the small extent of youth social participation may be the lack of spaces and situations that young people in the BHMR find for engaging in and learning about collective life and social participation. Without such experimentation it is difficult for them to believe that results can accrue from collective action.

By and large, there is no policy to stimulate youth participation by setting up mechanisms to facilitate their involvement in the classic institutions, such as political parties and trade unions. Party youth organizations, as well as the youth coordination offices or secretariats of certain municipalities in the BHMR, do not tend to generate languages and activities that come close to young people's world thereby reproducing the same defects as adult party organizations. There seems to be a lack of sensitivity in the adult world and its institutions in perceiving the world of young people and creating institutional spaces, in addition to school, that stimulate youth participation and the development of democratic values.

When the study examined the young people's school experience in greater depth, a number of issues and questions were raised about whether or not the institution plays a part in youth participation processes.

School, as said above, is one of the prime settings for learning forms and mechanisms of participation. However, in the Dialogue Groups we were struck by the fact that, with very few exceptions, young people did not mention student organizations, or even communicate demands or proposals relating to participation of that kind. This evidence is reinforced by the quantitative survey which revealed that most of the students were unaware of, and less than one fifth were active in student unions, class representatives and councils, and school councils.

Schools, both public and private, do not appear to have prioritized participation as an important dimension of the educational process. Nor have they even informed young people about their existence. One easy explanation to these data is to attribute the problem to the young students and consider them uninterested or apathetic. However, as pointed out above, when schools do offer activities that are different, students tend to get involved. At half the schools that do offer the activities mentioned earlier, there is significant participation by more than 60 per cent of students. In the Dialogue Groups, the young people visibly wanted to take part in the discussions and final evaluations. An important number of them expressed the wish to continue the discussions and to engage in some kind of group. It remains to be seen whether or not the existing school structure, teaching staff and school administration will organize to leverage that willingness to participate.

Many studies point to the need to flexibly organize time and space and to construct political and educational projects that dialogue with the people in school and not just with the administrative bodies. In the case of schools designed for poorer children who live day-to-day situations of deprivation, social inequality and unemployment, there is an even greater need for this flexibility. That is to say that education as a social right should not reproduce the same conditions and realities of people's lives which result from social inequalities. Nor should it reproduce the inequality bias between public and private, which has historically been an everyday part of life for Brazil's people. However, in day-to-day school relations, in the organization of curricula, in out-of-class activities and in participation opportunities, the right to education is not yet being exercised. Initiatives in this direction do exist, but they do not yet represent the majority of education measures.

Nonetheless, individuals continue to act within schools, bringing with them their values, representations, questions, behaviour and experiences. It is in that context that youth is a presence in school. Given all the limitations, young people continue their accidented or successful careers in public or private schools. They abandon the teaching institution or are abandoned by it, and/or even return to adult education programmes.

Schools relate with these concrete young people and with their potential for participation. As the institutions responsible for education and for socializing knowledge, schools are called on to internally redefine themselves on the basis of their relationship with young people. The study reveals that, despite significant initiatives taken in Brazil, this process of redefinition is slow and tense. It is taking place in the context of the human and educational tension within schools, which is permeated by class, race and gender biases and, in the specific case of this study, of youth as a stage of human life and by the condition of youth in this stage.

It is important to bear in mind that there is a relationship between enabling youth participation and the place that young people occupy in society, in the family and in public policies. On their own, schools are finding it difficult to build and rebuild significant means of participation. Schools compete and coexist with social projects, other times, youth cultural movements, subsistence needs, inequality, violence and the challenge of enabling effective citizenship. Schools do not always manage to take account of the dynamics and the changes produced in the formative settings that exist in present-day society. This is a complex process that young people are involved in.

Despite the challenges, schools cannot shirk their responsibility to change. Since they are among the few places that most of the young people in the survey pass through, the institution is challenged to build another type of organization for educational work and to review its participation arrangements, considering not just the adult world, but also the times of life it coexists with.

Schools are increasingly challenged and called on to look to people as individuals and not just to the structure in which they are inserted. When the focus is on the active individuals involved, then the structure of schools, how their work is organized, their day-to-day activities and their attitudes tend to be called into question. Through this process, new responses can begin to be developed and different educational practices constructed.

The study revealed that schools are not yet the ones wished and hoped for by young people, particularly poor young people, who were the majority in the Dialogue Groups. These young people are in the schools, however, and they need to be seen, heard and taken into consideration in a way that goes beyond the existing socially and culturally constructed youth stereotypes. Perhaps one way of actually turning eyes and ears to young people and their paths to participation is the avenue signalled by the study. It is not enough to 'discover' that, despite the problems, a portion of Brazil's youth goes to school. What we need to know is how and in what conditions they attend, by going beyond academic performance to investigate how youth construct the social networks and concrete means of participation that frame their lives inside and outside school.

What is it that schools have to learn from the challenge of youth participation? What can we understand about young people's disappointment with the traditional forms of political participation and the continual appeal by schools to that very type of participation? Do schools perceive that, to the great majority of young people, their participation seems depleted and no longer figures as a possible avenue for collective action? Do they perceive that a good number of young people end up investing in another type of path to participation? For these purposes, perhaps we ought to question the understanding and meaning of 'participation'. Constructed in their relationship with school, with society and with the ambiguity surrounding the real and effective exercise of social rights, young people point to other paths, to understanding differently, and to feeling differently. That process needs to be analyzed in greater depth.

References

Abramo, Helena Wendel & Branco, Pedro Paulo Martoni, *Retratos da Juventude Brasileira: análises de uma pesquisa nacional*, Editora Fundação Perseu Abramo, Instituto Cidadania (São Paulo, 2005).

Bendit, René, 'Participación social y política de los jóvenes en países de la Unión Europea', in Balardini, Sergio (Comp.), *La participación social y política de los jóvenes en el horizonte del nuevo siglo*, pp. 19-58, Flacso (Buenos Aires, 2000).

Brenner, Ana Karina, Carrano, Paulo & Dayrell, Juarez, 'Juventude brasileira: culturas do lazer e do tempo livre dos jovens brasileiros', in Abramo, Helena & Branco, Pedro Paulo Martoni, *Retratos da Juventude Brasileira: análises de uma pesquisa nacional*, Editora Fundação Perseu Abramo (São Paulo, 2005).

Dayrell, Juarez T, Gomes, Nilma L. & Leão, Geraldo M. P., *Relatório Preliminar dos Grupos de Diálogo. Região Metropolitana de Belo Horizonte*, Research Project *Juventude Brasileira e Democracia: participação, esferas e políticas públicas* (Belo Horizonte, June 2005).

Ibase, *Juventude brasileira e democracia: participação, esferas e políticas públicas*, mimeo (2004).

Ibase, *Relatório Global*. Research Project *Juventude brasileira e democracia: participação, esferas e políticas públicas*, Ibase & Pólis (Rio de Janeiro, Jan 2006).

Leccardi, Carmem, *Orizzonte del tempo: esperienza del tempo e mutamento sociale*, Franco Angeli (Milano, 1991).

Margulis, Mário, 'La juventud es más que una palabra', in Margulis, M. (Ed.), *La juventud es más que una palabra*, Editorial Biblos (Buenos Aires, 2000).

Melucci, Alberto, 'Juventude, tempo e movimentos sociais', *Juventude e contemporaneidade. Rev. Brasileira de Educação*, v, pp. 5-14, May-Aug/Sept-Dec, 1997, special edition, (São Paulo, 1997).

Morcellini, Mario, *Passagio al futuro: formazione e sociallizzazione tra vecchi e nuovi media*, Franco Angeli (Milan, 1997).

Pais, José Machado, *Culturas juvenis*, Imprensa Nacional Casa da Moeda (Lisboa, 1993).

—————————, *Ganchos, tachos e biscates: jovens, trabalho e futuro*, Âmbar (Lisboa, 2003).

Novaes, Regina & Mello, Cecília, *Jovens do Rio: circuitos, crenças e acessos, Comunicações do Iser*, xxi/57, Iser (Rio de Janeiro, 2002).

Peralva, Angelina, 'O jovem como modelo cultural', *Revista Brasileira de Educação*, v, vi (1997), Anped (São Paulo, 1997).

Sposito, Marilia, 'Algumas hipóteses sobre as relações entre movimentos sociais, juventude e educação', *Revista Brasileira de Educação*, xiii (2000), Anped (São Paulo, 2000).

Chapter 3

YOUTH, INFORMATION AND EDUCATION
Meanings on Television

Eliane Ribeiro*
Patrícia Lânes

In recent decades, using a variety of media it has been possible to call on an endless series of devices that have transformed the world into one vast network. At the same time as this network gives expression to a plethora of processes driving globalization, it also contributes to their establishment. Without a doubt, this communications apparatus facilitates diverse forms of encounters and dialogue, which are deployed according to what is to be communicated, to

---

* About the authors:
Eliane Ribeiro is a member of the overall *Juventude Brasileira e Democracia: participação, esferas e políticas públicas* study team. She has a Ph.D. in Education and postgraduate studies in Social and Educational Programme Evaluation (IDRC/IICA). Professor at Rio de Janeiro State University (Uerj) and with the postgraduate programme in Education at Rio de Janeiro State Federal University (Unirio).
Patrícia Lânes is a member of the overall *Juventude Brasileira e Democracia: participação, esferas e políticas públicas* study team. She is a journalist, specialist in Urban Sociology (Uerj), M.A. in Sociology, major in Anthropology (PPGSA/IFCS/UFRJ) and Ibase researcher.

whom, when and for what purpose. In this setting, it is evident that young people are fundamentally important players, because they generally learn, access and respond quicker to the ways in which we are communicating. Listening to them therefore appears to be a good way to try and understand the complex processes that are circulating through the field of communications.

At present in countries like Brazil, it is fundamentally important to have an in depth understanding of the role of the media – especially television – since it intersects with all kinds of young people. Television is a strong presence that, directly or indirectly, influences various dimensions of social life through subtle symbolic means. This fact alerts us to consider the set of ways that cultural goods are produced and broadcast to young Brazilians.

As Champagne warned (1999: 63), 'from now on the media is an integral part of reality or, if you prefer, produces effects on reality by creating a media view of reality that contributes to creating the reality it purports to describe'. Considering this series of concerns, it is only proper to look more carefully at whether information which discusses public affairs issues is accompanied by any kind of education that contributes to young people's civic participation.

The study *Brazilian Youth and Democracy: Participation, Spheres and Public Policies*, produced a striking set of data pointing to tensions in the relationship between information, education and media. The thinking offered here focuses on television, because 84.5 per cent of the 8,000 young people interviewed responded that they *obtain information on things that happen in the world* from television.

In that light, the challenge is to try to understand how far television reaches and what function it performs for various kinds of young people, supposing that 'the information and communication media construct meanings and act decisively in forming social subjects' (Fisher 1997: 60).

From among the various data and correlations available to us, we sought to relate what the young people declared to be their source of information on 'things that happen in the world', to their definition of acronyms and expressions reflecting various public debates. Some examples include: FTAA, ECA (Brazil's Statute on Children), World Social Forum, Greenpeace, NGOs, UN and quota policies.[1]

The data also permitted some assessment to be made of the relationship between television, information and education, in order to understand how far television has contributed to opening up young Brazilians' worldview, as well as their cultural and political universe.

Considering the enormous number of people who access television and the astonishing amount of time they spend watching and listening to it, we are required to think about television and its formative role. Still, it remains a challenge to answer Adorno's classic question: what effects does television have on people after all?

Far from yielding definitive answers, the data examined here raise new questions, especially because they entail thinking about how young people use television. Children, young people and adults, whose lives are packed, day after day with images, weave new experiences and new ways of seeing the world and themselves through these images (Salgado, Ribes & Jobim e Souza 2005). Contemporary culture may perhaps find its most intense form of expression in images. Their uses, however, are various and can permeate information, entertainment and education, depending on the conditions that young people are subject to, such as social class, sex, race/ethnicity, schooling, place of residence and so on.

In this regard, public opinion cannot be indifferent to what happens on TV in terms of entertainment, information and education. The question that arises is: how can we manage to expand television's enlightening effects so as to help build a better world? In this way, thinking about youth means also thinking about the media.

How they obtain information

In order to advance our understanding of how young people in Brazil's metropolitan regions construct their cultural habits, we asked whether they try to stay informed about what is happening in the world. The answer was affirmative from 85.8 per cent of the interviewees. The most significant differences appeared according to class: while 91.9 per cent of young people in classes A/B responded that they try to stay informed, the percentage falls to 80.9 per cent in classes D/E.

A similar difference emerges in relation to schooling. Of those youth who had completed middle schooling or more, 93 per cent responded that they try to stay informed about what is happening in the world. Of those with less schooling (youth who had not completed fundamental schooling), the percentage fell to 75.2 per cent.

This inequality was repeated with similar emphasis between young people who attended private schools and those at public schools with 94 per cent of the former responding that they were informed about what happens in the world, while among the latter group, the number fell to 84.6 per cent. From this data it is possible to conclude that there is a tendency for young people in classes A/B with more schooling and at private schools to consider themselves informed.

Those who answered in the affirmative were then asked what media they used most to stay informed. The majority said they used television (84.5 per cent), followed by newspapers and print magazines (57.1 per cent), radio (49 per cent), then friends, 'the gang' and colleagues at work (28 per cent), Internet (27 per cent), families (18 per cent), school friends (18 per cent) and teachers (14.4 per cent).

Table 1 – Sources and media used by young people to stay informed (percentage –multiple responses)

Usual information sources and media	Percentage of youth
Television	84.5
Newspapers/print magazines	57.1
Radio	49.0
Friends/"the gang"/colleagues at work	28.0
Internet	27.0
Families	18.0
School friends	15.0
Teachers	14.4
Other	4.4
Don't know/No opinion	0.1

Source: Ibase/Pólis, *Juventude Brasileira e Democracia: participação, esferas e políticas públicas*, 2005.

Television thus predominates as the medium through which young people, regardless of class, colour, sex, schooling or any other attribute, gain access to information. However, there are differences between the other media considered. Among young people in classes A/B, for example, the Internet appears in third place among the ways they stay informed, outranked by only television and newspapers and print magazines. Meanwhile, among classes D/E, the Internet ranks eighth which is evidence of a lack of digital inclusion affecting poor youth. Among young people who had completed middle school or higher, the Internet ranks fourth at around 39 per cent. Finally, among those who completed no more than fundamental schooling, the Internet ranks eighth, informing only 10.2 per cent.

There is a need to think about the role of schools as information sources, bearing in mind how school friends and teachers ranked in this overall picture. This is especially important when we consider the evident differences in the media that young people from different classes and with differing degrees of schooling use to access information. It is also significant when we consider the television's unchallenged predominance as a way of staying informed.

Although a little more than half the young people (52.9 per cent) were not studying at the time of the survey, all had been to school and, nonetheless, classmates and, particularly, teachers hardly figure as sources of information. Therefore it is possible to ask: what role is school, represented in the question by teachers and colleagues, fulfilling in the lives of young Brazilians? More specifically, how are teachers building their relationship with the young people who are at school? Is it possible that school, which should be the key formative institution, is not recognized as a way to access information?

The media therefore appears to be the main source of information for metropolitan youth in Brazil. Although we need to think about what information is being given, we also need to take account of the mediating role that young people are playing in accessing the information provided. We must also think about how friends, colleagues, families and teachers can play a central role in this mediation – and how capable young people feel accessing different media not only as spectators, but also as producers of information.

When asked whether they collaborated with any communication medium, the majority said no. That is to say, 78 per cent of the young people had never collaborated on a school newspaper, fanzines, radio show, community TVs or newspapers or even in making videos. The other side of the story, however, is that 13.8 per cent (1,104 interviewees) collaborate or had at some point collaborated on a school newspaper; 3.2 per cent, with a community newspaper; 2.5 per cent, with community radio; 2.4 per cent, with fanzines, 1.9 per cent, in producing videos; and 1.1 per cent, with community TV.

This shows that, although teachers and school friends are possible interlocutors, they are not valued as sources of or channels to access information. However, it is through school and one of its media, the newspaper, that most of the young people who report collaborating or having collaborated manage to produce or share information, thereby moving from the role of recipient to producer.

Once again, this engagement does not occur homogeneously among young people when differentiated by class, age, sex, colour, schooling and place of residence. The youngest collaborate or have collaborated slightly more with school newspapers (16.5 per cent) than the other age groups. Participation in community newspapers, however, increases with age (15 to 17 years old – 2.6 per cent; 18 to 20 years old – 3.1 per cent; 21 to 24 years old – 3.6 per cent). Class differences continue to hold, regardless of the medium in question, as can be seen below in Table 2.

Table 2 – Young people's participation in media, by social class (percentage)

Medium	Overall	A/B	C	D/E
School newspaper	13.8	16.4	13.3	12.4
Community newspaper	3.2	4.6	3.1	2.1
Community radio	2.5	3.5	2.4	2.1
Fanzines	2.4	3.0	2.1	2.1
Producing videos	1.9	3.9	1.6	0.9

Source: Ibase/Pólis, *Juventude Brasileira e Democracia: participação, esferas e políticas públicas*, 2005.

In order to better understand the relationship between information reception and production, other aspects of the process must be considered, albeit in general terms. As regards both information received and information produced, opportunities arise very unequally for young people from different social classes, levels of schooling and type of school.

A public policy designed for young people must provide not only alternative ways to access and communicate with young people, but also differentiated opportunities for youth to voice their opinions and demands. Serious consideration must be given to mass and alternative media, particularly television, when formulating a cultural policy to broadly contemplate Brazilian youth.

How they understand reality

In order to discover the quality of the information received by the young people, keeping in mind that 85.8 per cent claimed to be informed about what happens in the world, they were asked the meanings of seven acronyms and expressions of very different kinds. These were FTAA, ECA (Brazil's Statute on Children), World Social Forum, Greenpeace, NGOs, UN and quota policies.

The choice of acronyms and expressions makes it possible to gauge the quality of information on international politics (FTAA and UN), social rights (ECA and quota policy) and about organized civil society (World Social Forum, NGOs and Greenpeace). For the same purpose, but focussing on Brazilian politics, they were asked to name the mayor of the city where they lived, the governor of their state and the President of Brazil.

Knowledge of the acronyms and expressions in the first block of questions was extremely poor. In order of correct answers, 30.4 per cent were able to give the meaning of UN; 21.5 per cent of NGOs; 15.8 per cent of FTAA; 9 per cent of

Greenpeace; 3 per cent of quota policies; 2.8 per cent of ECA; and only 2 per cent of World Social Forum.

Table 3 – Young people who correctly answered the meaning of selected acronyms and expressions (percentage)

Acronym/Expression	Percentage of young people
UM	30.4
NGOs	21.5
FTAA	15.8
Greenpeace	9
Quota policies	3
ECA	2.8
World Social Forum	2

Source: Ibase/Pólis, *Juventude Brasileira e Democracia: participação, esferas e políticas públicas*, 2005.

The exposure given to the issues to which these expressions relate in the mass media, the quality of information the young people have access to and/or how interested they are in that information may explain why most of the young people could not define the acronyms and expressions.

When young people, and most people, watch television, read newspapers and magazines, listen to the radio or talk to friends and family, they do not grasp everything which is said, shown or talked about. There is a constant selection process that has to do with the life history of the individual involved in the communication process, the social context they find themselves in and what – consciously or not – they believe makes a difference in their lives. This, however, does not exempt the media from producing responsible, quality information that shares different points of view on the issue addressed, thereby giving the public more opportunity to form its opinion on the issues covered in an autonomous and democratic way.

However, it is important to draw attention to the fact that there are complexities to the communication process. Among these is the fact that the subject, in this case the young person, does not receive information passively, but rather grasps some information better, after mediation and elaboration at various levels. The acronyms UN and FTAA, which ranked, respectively first and third, have had a firm presence in the media for some time (particularly UN). In a period relatively close to the interview, the FTAA was the subject of a referendum throughout Brazil, which may have improve its score among those surveyed.

The acronym NGOs, which ranked second, has been very widespread in the last decade not just in information circulating in the mass media, but also in poor neighbourhoods, *favelas* and peripheral areas. Since the 1990s, NGOs have come to form part of many young people's daily lives. Even if they do not directly take part in their activities, they have at least heard of them.

According to Sergio Haddad, chairman of the Brazilian Association of NGOs from 2000 to 2003, 'NGOs are numerous, hard to count. (…) Since the Rio-92 Environment Conference, NGOs have become a presence in the media and in public debate' (*Caros Amigos* magazine, November 2002). Greenpeace, which is also an NGO and ranked fourth, carries out spectacular actions which are featured in the media, and has spent several decades engaged in exploits of this kind. In addition, for the last few years, environment-related issues have formed part of the school curriculum (LDB – Law No. 9394/96), which may contribute to drawing young people's attention to this subject.

Quota policies (3 per cent), the ECA (2,8 per cent) and the World Social Forum (2 per cent) ranked lowest. Despite the very recent, prominent national controversy over whether quota policies are workable and necessary, particularly at public universities, the meaning of these policies may still be abstract and unclear to most people. Although poor, black youth may be the main beneficiaries of quota policies, understanding of the term on the part of young people follows the same trend as described above. It was the younger, single, childless, white youth from classes A/B, with most schooling who attended private schools, who were most able to define the term.

It was after the survey ended, and particularly in 2006, that the media began to cover the debate over social and racial quotas as a mechanism for reserving places at public universities. Arguments for and against quotas appear recurrently, even though – especially racial – quotas were given most prominence when the issue first arose.

Government policies on ethnic and racial issues have been institutionalized in Brazil through the Special Secretariat for Racial Equality Policies (*Secretaria Especial de Políticas de Promoção da Igualdade Racial*, Seppir), which has also helped make this debate more visible. It can be inferred that if the survey were carried out now, more young people would recognize the expression and be able to give its meaning correctly.[2]

The Statute on Children (ECA) represents a victory on the part of social movements from the early 1990s. Although it is an important legal mechanism guaranteeing the rights of young people up to 18 years of age, it continues to be unknown to most of these beneficiaries. This is very likely because the media did not cover it widely at the time of the survey, nor has it been widely publicized, particularly among the young people who could most benefit from it, such as the poor. The data indicate that young people in classes D/E are those who least knew what it meant (1.2 per cent), as well as those who attended public schools (2.3 per cent), with the percentage rising to 6.1 per cent among those who attended private schools.

Lastly, the least-known expression was the World Social Forum, which may still be considered a recent phenomenon. Although the Forum's participants were largely young people, with 37.7 per cent of registered attendees between 14 and 24 years old in 2003, it remains a localized event. It appears annually in the media since 2001 when it was first held as a world event in Porto Alegre, Rio Grande do Sul.

In addition, participant profiling (2003) showed that it continued to be an elite gathering (36.2 per cent of the participants had been to university and 27.5 per cent had graduated) of social movement militants and organized civil society more generally (64.9 per cent of participants in 2003 belonged to a social movement or organization). Its impact and visibility continue to be restricted to those people in or close to the social movements universe.

When asked to name the President of Brazil, the governor of the state and the mayor of the city where they lived, most respondents (92.6 per cent) answered the first correctly; while 75.3 per cent were able to name the governor of their state and 85.8 per cent, the mayor of their city. It should be noted that the survey was conducted during an electoral year (2004) and period (October-November), which may have influenced the high number of correct answers.

Some trends, nonetheless, may be identified. One is that the young people have more information about what, in their view, may affect their lives most directly. Since Brazil is a country where politics is highly personalized - with much of the population voting for the person rather than the party, for instance – young people may recognize their representatives in the Executive Branch of Government (which is more highly valued than other powers) as the cause of their problems and look to them for possible solutions.

Beyond television

Although television figures as are the key source of information, when we examine the group of young people who gave the correct meaning of a variety of acronyms and expressions separately, television no longer appears so important, as shown in the table below.

Table 4 – Young people who answered the definition of acronyms and expressions correctly, by source or medium where they obtain information (percentage)

	FTAA	ECA	World Social Forum	Green peace	NGO	UN	Quota policies
Friends	3.3	6.5	4.5	18.7	47.8	68.4	67.4
Family	35.3	7.2	4.5	19.8	51.2	71.6	65.9
Internet	42.5	8.7	7.2	30.6	58.1	71.3	70.8
Newspapers/Magazines	39.1	7.4	6.2	24.2	51.0	67.0	67.4
Teachers	42.9	10.8	6.0	25.6	55.5	70.9	64.5
Radio	34.8	7.9	6.3	21.9	48.6	66.3	66.6
Television	35.9	6.7	5.0	22.3	47.8	65.9	63.3

Source: Ibase/Pólis, *Juventude Brasileira e Democracia: participação, esferas e políticas públicas*, 2005.

In the table above, it can be seen that the young people who correctly identified the acronyms and expressions use other sources to obtain information about the world. The three most cited sources are Internet, teachers, and newspapers and magazines.

The sources of information mentioned by young people from classes A/B, on all the subjects were: newspapers and magazines, Internet and radio. These young people provided the highest number of correct answers on NGO, UN and quota policies. The situation is quite different when compared with the young people from classes D/E, that is, the poorest sector. In this case, the Internet is mentioned in relation to all subjects, followed by family, and newspapers and magazines. The poorest young people provided the most correct answers on the meanings of.

The situation with regard to young people from class C is rather interesting and deserves further attention. In this case teachers play a prevalent role in practically all of the subjects, followed by the Internet and newspapers and magazines. Television does not appear as a major source of information on any of the subjects involved. Young people from class C also demonstrated a level of information well above that of the young people from classes D/E.

Final remarks

The data presented here intends to be the basis for preliminary thinking on how far the information that young people report receiving via television has been adequate (more than informing and entertaining) for contributing to sound knowledge about what is happening in the world.

The young people generally show little understanding of the meaning of expressions related to public affairs. Although they report getting their information from TV, when called on to qualify that information, we observe the use of other sources, such as the Internet, even if superficially. Teachers are another reference mentioned, especially by the middle classes. Schooling level is another strong influence affecting whether young people call on other networks to access knowledge.

Although young people claim television to be their primary source of information, it can be inferred that this fact is not directly related to whether or not they understand what is reported there. After all, watching television is not necessarily an exclusive activity. Studies show that young people watch television while they study, listen to music, talk on the telephone and so on.

Also fitting here is the way television broadcasts public events, because often, although they are given exhaustive coverage, they are presented superficially. They are also submerged in an astounding welter of information pouring out in a series of images selected and edited by media companies.

Thought should also be given to the importance of constructing other ways of watching television, to denaturalize what is profoundly familiar to us. School would be one of the prime locations[3] for this, however organizations engaged in democratizing society can also play a leading role by exploring people's understanding of the media, what goes on behind the scenes, the ways information circulates and the relationship between ratings and the editorial function.

There is no doubt that television needs to be questioned both politically and sociologically about its images, sounds and its relationships (Bourdieu 1997: 12). However, since it is situated in a given context, the question arises: to what point could television be that different from the society it is part of? As Novaes warns,

> Television is permeated by the tensions and contradictions of Brazil. And I think that, just as young people are society's rear-view mirror, so young people mirror us, they are not different. Because the phase of youth is a time of experimentation, a time when identity is being created, television can also be a thermometer in that regard. (Novaes 2006)

It therefore seems that television is mainly performing an entertainment function, occupying young people's idle moments, and making a limited contribution to their political and cultural education. Although we know that information goes beyond the plane of the simple transmission of facts, it is clear that the use of TV as entertainment alone adds little to stimulate more complex thinking about the needs of the world we live in.

As Adorno has already warned (1997), a television 'habit' is developing where television, like other mass media, is becoming the only stated content of information. Through the abundance of what it offers, it is diverting young people's understanding from other agents present in the process of their education. We must make a detached appraisal of this utilization of symbols; discovering that would contribute to our better understanding of exactly what space television has taken up in the lives of the new generations.

If information cannot be divorced from education, it is fundamental to think about the communications media in public policy terms, so that the space that television occupies in our societies can contribute to prompt critical thinking or, as Bourdieu stresses, to prevent television, which 'could have been a formidable instrument for direct democracy, from turning into an instrument of symbolic oppression' (1997: 13). It is therefore essential for societies not to shirk the specific and extremely serious responsibility of shaping new generations, informed above all by critical thinking about one of these key agencies - television.

References

Adorno, Theodor, Televisão e formação, http://www.educacaoonline.pro.br/art_televisao_e_formacao.asp?f_id_artigo=524. Translation: Wolfgang Leo.

Bourdieu, Pierre, *Sobre a televisão*, Jorge Zahar Ed. (Rio de Janeiro, 1997).

Champagne, Patrick, 'A Visão Mediática', in *A miséria do mundo*, Pierre Bourdieu (coord.), Editora Vozes (Petrópolis, 1999).

Fischer, Rosa M. B., 'O estatuto pedagógico da mídia: questões de análise'. *Educação e Realidade*, xxii/ii (1997), pp. 59-79, (Porto Alegre, 1997).

Haddad, Sergio, Interview in *Caros Amigos magazine*, November 2002.

Ibase & Pólis, *Relatório nacional de pesquisa de opinião*. Research Project *Juventude Brasileira e democracia: participação, esferas e políticas públicas*, Ibase, Pólis (March 2005).

Ibase & Secretaria Executiva do Fórum Social Mundial, 'Pesquisa sobre o perfil dos participantes', *Coleção Fórum Social Mundial 2003*, volume V, Ibase (Rio de Janeiro, 2003).

Novaes, Regina, Round table on youth and media. UFRGS. Canal Futura/Rede Globo, Porto Alegre. Accessed on 13 November 2006. http://www.intercom.org.br/boletim/a02n40/acontece_futura.shtml.

Salgado, Raquel Gonçalves, Pereira, Rita Marisa Ribes & Jobim e Souza, Solange, 'Pela tela, pela janela: questões teóricas e práticas sobre infância e televisão', *Cadernos Cedes*, xxv, lxv (Campinas, 2005). Available at: <http://www.scielo.br/scielo.php?script=sci_arttext&pid=S0101-32622005000100002&lng=en&nrm=iso>. Accessed on 24 April 2007. Prepublication.

Chapter 4

DEBATING THE DIALOGUE METHODOLOGY

Livia De Tommasi*
Suzanne Taschereau
Nilton Bueno Fischer
Gustavo Venturi

In recent years, there has been growing interest in the subject of youth in Brazil. It has entered the public policy agendas of local, state and federal governments and is also of interest to the media and a focus for intervention by NGOs and business foundations.

---

* About the authors:
 Livia De Tommasi is the regional supervisor of the study Juventude Brasileira e Democracia in the Recife metropolitan region. She holds a Ph.D. in Sociology.
 Suzanne Taschereau is a collaborator on the Brazil-Canada project and in the National Youth Dialogue in Canada. Senior advisor & research associate, consultant with the Canadian Policy Research Networks (CPRN).
 Nilton Bueno Fischer is the regional supervisor of the study in the Porto Alegre metropolitan region. He is a Professor at the Centro Universitário Lasalle, collaborates with the PPG/EDU/UFRGS and is a CNPq researcher.
 Gustavo Venturi holds a Ph.D. in Political Science and is director of the research advisory institute Criterium Assessoria em Pesquisas.

Events that took place between 2003 and 2005 demonstrate that the subject has come to the centre of public agendas. These included public hearings and state and national seminars which were called to pursue discussions of a National Youth Plan, to be drafted by the Chamber of Deputies' Special Commission on Youth; the installation of an inter-ministerial commission to study federal government action on youth matters; the installation of a National Youth Secretariat and National Youth Council at the federal level; and an increase in the number of municipal and state advisory, coordinating and managerial bodies directed specifically to youth.

There is also a growing perception of how important it is to support these processes with research data and analyses on the realities facing Brazilian youth. A mechanism is needed to highlight young people's demands and needs, and how and where they express and organize themselves, in order to broaden the picture painted by census studies traditionally carried out by the Brazilian Institute of Geography and Statistics (IBGE).

This sets the context for the initiative by two Brazilian NGOs, *Instituto Brasileiro de Análises Sociais e Econômicas* (Ibase), in Rio de Janeiro, and *Instituto de Estudos, Formação e Assessoria em Políticas Sociais* (Pólis), in São Paulo. They worked in partnership with a Canadian organization, Canadian Policy Research Networks (CPRN), and the Brazilian government, with sponsorship and financial support from Canada's International Development Research Center (IDRC). The idea was to conduct a comprehensive diagnostic study of the forms, content and meanings of social and political participation by young Brazilians between the ages of 14 and 24.

The focus on participation was designed to counter the view, which is widely reported in the media, that young people in contemporary societies and in Brazil in particular, are 'apathetic', and do not participate in political affairs, or engage in social struggles for larger causes. Convinced that youth participation is strategically important for consolidating the process of democratization of Brazilian society, the proponent organizations used a theoretical frame of reference based on the knowledge of specialists in the field. In recent decades, these specialists have stressed the importance of new forms of youth participation and new ways in which they express their demands in the public sphere. These specialists include authors such as Helena Abramo, Marilia Sposito and Paulo Carrano, in Brazil, and Leslie Serna, Miguel Abad and Rossana Reguillo, in other Latin American countries.

The study *Brazilian Youth and Democracy: Participation, Spheres and Public Policies* was carried out in seven of Brazil's metropolitan regions (Belém, Recife, Salvador, Belo Horizonte, São Paulo, Rio de Janeiro and Porto Alegre) and in the Federal District, through a network of local partners, mostly nongovernmental organizations and academic institutions. The most significant novelty and challenge – besides the specific subject focus – lay in applying the *Choice Work Dialogue* methodology for the first time in Brazil. This methodology was developed by Canadian groups and is known in Brazil as 'Dialogue Groups'.

In the democratic system, leaders must take decisions in the light of citizen opinions, values and needs, and their ways of discussing problems and dealing with opportunities in their communities. The Dialogue seeks the most convincing arguments in favour of certain directional changes, that is to say, about what part of the political sphere is susceptible to change.

The Dialogue situation allows people to provide their opinions in dialogue with the opinions of others. In this regard, the method has both research and educational value, and even hopes to prompt changes in the ways citizens think and position themselves with regard to social realities. The methodology can therefore be considered part of the action-research tradition that has so strongly marked the Brazilian social movement activities.

The Dialogue makes it possible to identify what options are possible in addressing a given problem by asking what citizens are willing to do or to accept as a result of their choices. Through the exchange of points of view, the Dialogue is at the same time informative and an interchange intent on producing more refined judgments and values to guide decision-making.

In Brazil, a total of 913 young people participated in the five Dialogue Groups held in each metropolitan region surveyed. These young participants were selected from among respondents who filled in a questionnaire during the first stage of the study. The questionnaire was designed to sketch an overall profile of Brazilian youth's situation, specifically regarding schooling, work, access to culture and leisure, and participation.

In Brazil the Dialogues lasted one day (the Dialogue Day), during which a sequence of methodological steps was systematically followed. First the goals of the study and of the responsible organizations were presented. Then the participants were introduced and the pre- and post-Dialogue questionnaires were handed out. The participants were then split into subgroups of at most ten members. Together, these groups read the Manual (Dialogue template) which contains key information on the subject of the Dialogue and on the three *Caminhos Participativos* (Paths to Participation) proposed (the path of participating in social movements, political parties or trade unions; the path of volunteer work; and the path of participating in informal youth groups), with arguments for and against each type of participation. The groups then presented their work to the plenary session. Participants were then able to jointly identify a set of similarities and differences in the various presentations and explore the consequences of the choices made. Finally, the Day was brought to a conclusion and evaluated.

In order to adapt the methodology to the Brazilian situation, a CD-ROM was prepared to present the content of the Manual in clear, accessible, enjoyable language. In the morning, participants were supposed to dialogue about 'the Brazil we want', in answer to the question: 'Thinking about the life you lead as a young Brazilian, what could improve in education, work, and culture and leisure activities?'. After agreeing on what improvements they wanted, these improvements would serve as a frame of reference for the afternoon Dialogue. In the afternoon the guiding question was: 'Thinking about what you listed this morning on what should improve in education, work, culture and leisure in Brazil, how are you willing to participate in order to help these improvements come about?'

The Dialogues were professionally facilitated by educators tasked with facilitating the course of the Dialogue by providing information and moderating the discussions. The Dialogues were also registered and monitored by observer-researchers who were responsible for recording significant situations and behaviour. On the basis of this material, each local team of researchers prepared a report commenting on the results obtained. Then the central team responsible for the study – after discussions with all the researchers involved – drew up an overall report that was widely circulated among public policy-makers, researchers and the general public electronically, in print and through the audiovisual media.

It was a considerable challenge applying the methodology in Brazil, not only because it was being done for the first time, but because it needed to be applied simultaneously in several places by different teams of researchers and facilitators. These teams had to embrace the methodology and try to suit it to Brazilian realities. Accordingly, when the report was being produced for publication, two researchers (Livia De Tommasi, regional project supervisor in the Recife metropolitan region, and Nilton Bueno Fischer, supervisor in the Porto Alegre metropolitan region) decided to engage in a dialogue with one of the CPRN consultants, Suzanne Taschereau, and a Brazilian research specialist, Gustavo Venturi (responsible for conducting other studies on the situation of Brazilian youth in recent years). They did so in order to explore certain aspects of the methodology application in Brazil in greater depth and analyze these critically on the basis of the comments contained in the regional reports.

In order to be consistent with the proposed methodology, which centres on participants expressing their opinions, respecting the opinions of others and dialoguing with them, this text maintains the original format of our dialogue. Also, the distances separating the people involved precluded any face to face dialogue, which would have enabled us to produce a collective text.

The outcome of this virtual conversation on the methodology and the outcomes of the Brazilian Dialogues on youth and democracy can be found below.

Conversation on the Dialogues

LIVIA: To start with, I would like to single out what I consider the greatest potential and at the same time the greatest challenge, of the Dialogue methodology. It pursues three goals at the same time. These are: 1) to educate citizens, both in terms of learning new content (the information provided on the subject of the study) and fostering a space for dialogue, listening and thinking; 2) to deliberate on choices and their consequences with a view to influencing public policies, that is, exercising democracy; 3) and to carry out research.

Can these three dimensions be combined in a single process? How do you prevent one goal from taking precedence over the others, thereby invalidating their results? In the course of our conversation, so as to stimulate our dialogue, I will be referring to remarks made by researchers responsible for the study in Brazil, which bring out contradictions, difficulties and possibilities that surfaced in applying the methodology.

SUZANNE: This is an issue we faced in Canada too. What we saw in practice leads us to believe that the three goals can be attained and what's more, they can reinforce one another. For example, the research can reinforce the educational goal, by feeding into the Manual with data expressed in opinion polls on the issues that concern young people and on what action is possible. For example, the link between education and employment, the demographic trends, how public policy decisions are taken and so on. Thus, the goal of educating citizens is reinforced by empirical data gathered by the quantitative first stage of the study.

However, there may be tensions between pursuing the goals of education/reflection and deliberation. For example, the need for rigorous comparative research may limit the possibility of adjusting the content of the deliberative process from one region to another.

There is therefore a creative tension among these three goals and the actors pursuing them. As an animator/facilitator, my main concern is for the young people who take part in the Dialogue to have a positive experience of the democratic process: for them to go home having learned something, to be 'turned on' by the Dialogue experience and by discovering the values they share with others and the possible courses of action that may open up. To my researcher colleagues, the methodology and the analyses are the most important concerns. It is through dialoguing among ourselves and by thinking critically that we improve how we do things in practice.

Note that the main goal of the Dialogues we held in Canada was to create a public space where young people, as citizens, can:

- learn together about some of the issues that concern them (health, education, how decisions are taken) and which also represent a public policy concern;

- exchange ideas on what values should guide public policy choices and to deliberate on these choices and their consequences for them as social actors;

- identify the roles they are willing to play (and how they want to play them) and what they expect of actors responsible for improving their lives (governments, private sector etc.).

Unfortunately, very often agencies will not fund post-Dialogue follow-up studies. In Canada, we managed to do it once with surprising results (a significant percentage of citizens identified the Dialogue as an importance influence on their lives or their active civic engagement). It would be interesting to be able to explore what influence the study and the report you have written have had on decision-makers and young people, six or twelve months later.

NILTON: We should remember that the things the young people say during the Dialogue Group process are connected in one way or another with their 'prior' situations. Therefore, the data collected do not reflect 'raw' information or purely reactions to the 'research moment'. Therefore we can gauge the dimensions of possible continuities, new knowledge that they acquired (multiple learnings) during the Dialogue Day, developments in their respective 'social environments' (experiences in the family, at school, in groups of whatever kind – musical, sporting, political, religious etc.).

For the purpose of evaluating the repercussions of this methodology, impact is gauged using a broader approach where it is related to young people's lives rather than considered a result from an activity dissociated from their practices and experiences. During the period of research, the three dimensions are contemplated as an interconnected process and, at the same time, as a connection with the lives of those young people, before and after the experience.

GUSTAVO: I would like to reaffirm my admiration for this methodology and for the processes and challenges embedded in it. At the same time, recall that doing applied research means making a succession of choices, all with their pros and cons. In this case, the tension among the proposed goals takes a reasonable toll on the survey's validity in terms of the *how far the results can be generalized*. As 'the intention from the outset was to perceive how Brazilian youth, considered in all its diversity and complexity, would be willing to occupy the democratic public sphere',[1] it seems relevant to me to discuss how far results can be generalized.

The young people who participated in the Dialogue Groups were all drawn exclusively from Brazil's metropolitan regions, so the survey's representativeness must be delimited to the population actually studied – and that goes for interpretation of the quantitative research as well. Even without going into the merits of the criteria for selecting the Dialogue participants, at best the survey results offer insights into metropolitan youth.

This is not to play down the project's importance – with 8,000 interviews and 39 Dialogue Groups in seven metropolitan regions and the Federal District, it is extremely valuable in itself – but rather to be clear about the limits inherent to the sample designs chosen.

The national survey by *Instituto Cidadania* that resulted in the publication *Retratos da Juventude Brasileira*[2] brought out some contrasts between young people in the big cities and in medium and small towns in the interior, that is to say between urban and rural youth. These contrasts relate to young people's willingness to do volunteer work, their perception of institutional channels of participation, and the nature of the self-managed groups they engage in, which are the paths for participation proposed in our Dialogue Groups. We should not disregard these issues when talking about the diversity of youth.

LIVIA: I think Suzanne made an important point regarding the division of tasks among the study team. Having a multidisciplinary team made up of specialists from different fields, each responsible for one dimension of the process in depth, may help keep those dimensions (research, deliberation and education) separate and address the challenges intrinsic in pursuing each goal more objectively. Each specialist can alert colleagues to possible biases that may be caused by not distinguishing these three dimensions clearly. In that regard, I think that the observer – who in this case is responsible for the research dimension – plays just as important a role as the dialogue animator (the educator/facilitator). It is also important to prepare objective instruments to record observations, and they should be common to all teams. 'How' the participants speak is probably just as important as 'what' they have to say.

Nonetheless, the question remains: when subjects are placed in a research situation and prompted to discuss a specific theme, can they at the same time reach conclusions and 'ponder' what is the best course of action to follow? Inversely, when subjects are prompted to deliberate, make choices and take decisions, can they at the same time be research 'informants'? The two processes are quite different in nature. It would be interesting to learn more about what happens in focus groups. I would like to hear from Gustavo on that.

GUSTAVO: I think the answer to both questions is yes. There are no – nor should there be any – ready-made packages of research methods and techniques capable of dealing with any object and goal. The creativity of the methodology in question is a good example of how that necessary freedom can be exercised and the fruits which can result. However, just as in any act of legitimate freedom, you must not lose sight of the consequences of each choice you make.

In this case, the participant selection criteria, the laboratory setting for data collection and the instruments prepared in advance with a view to making the Dialogue dynamics work, all conditioned the results and the range of possible deliberations, although it is impossible to discern to what extent. Even if participants were offered the option of constructing new scenarios or paths to participation, interviewing is full of examples of the inductive power that stimulated choices exert over final choices to the detriment of original suggestions. For the latter to prevail, participants must have a reasonable degree of autonomy and/or prior experience – in practice or thinking – with the issues in question.

If there is prior consensus among the organizers about the deliberations on the suggested paths, and if that is important for the subsequent, politically key purpose of impacting impact ongoing public policy-making, then a choice was made that put deliberation before research.

My hypothesis is that we would see differences in the research results if, for example, the Manual distributed at the start of the dynamics was followed not by a presentation of the scenarios (which is a substantive and necessarily leading stimulus), but rather by opening remarks from each participant 'spontaneously' expressing their main concerns on the issue in question.

That would have made it possible to control a result that would be more generalizable to the surveyed population such as the group's opinions on the envisaged paths to participation for example. However, having been influenced by pre-existing scenarios (and by the presupposition of the project's designers that participation is intrinsically good), they do not represent exactly what metropolitan youth think about participation, but what they would tend to think if they were all subject to the same scenarios in groups with profiles and educational dynamics similar to those of our Dialogue.

LIVIA: 'It was very difficult for most of the young people to express their opinions on a subject they had probably never stopped to think about. Even more so since the way the question was formulated implied the need to draw on a readiness for action (and not just to give an opinion). *"How are you all willing to participate?"* presupposes a willingness to participate in something and, at the same, the ability to choose.'[3]

SUZANNE: That really is a major challenge. Citizens, including young people, get involved to the extent that they are brought face to face with issues that affect them. The central questions of the Dialogue must be relevant to young people's daily lives and be a concern to them. The subjects of employment, education, mental health and violence concern them. The themes of the Dialogue can be identified and formulated by polling a smaller number of young people before the Dialogue, so as to ensure that the participation question ties in with something concrete that young people would like to act on. Being able or unable to act is probably connected with how difficult it is to imagine the possibilities. If the researchers have already worked with young people to identify possible courses of action that are present in society and that young people are already involved in, then it is possible to stimulate them to think about the advantages and limits of that model of action and about the possible alternatives.

GUSTAVO: I don't think the fact that it was the first time many of them had stopped to think, and the clichés they repeated as a result, are factors that invalidate their opinions. Rather, they should be considered as starting points for the Dialogues. I'm assuming the facilitators had the resources and time to explore these issues and will have helped bring out the latent discourses underlying the discourses initially manifested in embarrassing situations. Meanwhile, the expectation implicit in the Dialogue's setting a high value on participation may have forced responses that the young people felt were expected of them, particularly as no prior provision was made for it to be called into question.

On the other hand, it is possible to find ways to lessen the constraint. For example, if some groups contained just participants with prior experience and others just participants with no prior experience, then the dynamics could have developed at paces of their own. Some groups would spend longer discussing the importance of whether or not to participate; others would take it as given and more quickly move on to discussing the various paths.

LIVIA: Few of them took the opportunity to speak, particularly during the plenary session. Those who did so generally had more public speaking experience, and deployed discursive repertoires that spoke of their activities as – mainly political party, religious or student – militants. Others marshalled repertoires connected to family life and experiences.

NILTON: I agree that different histories, experiences and realities strongly influence what people put into words during the Dialogue. For a more enlightening analysis of the Dialogue Groups, it is important to understand what young people say and do in their respective contexts. Some members of the groups found it difficult to speak out during the deliberations, which were dominated by those who spoke most, and several young people said nothing at all. This was the same in all metropolitan regions in Brazil. Even if the issues are of interest to all the study participants and are legitimatized by the literature on youth, it is up to the researchers to think critically about these group reactions, both of 'domination' and of inhibition (silence).

GUSTAVO: I suspect that the groups' heterogeneity – in terms of social background more than prior experience of participation – may have contributed to making it difficult for some of the participants to express themselves. As I understood it, selection of Dialogue participants contemplated the 'diverse social classes and levels of schooling' that are characteristic of Brazilian metropolitan youth – which is a legitimate concern if the study is to be representative.

Another thing that seems to have happened – accidentally or deliberately, I don't know – was that this diversity was reproduced in each group in the Dialogue. That is a procedure that goes against the practical experience accumulated in group discussions or focus groups. A relative degree of homogeneity among the participants is both decisive in reducing inhibitions and helping the discussion flow and is half way to ensuring that the majority participate (which always depends partly on the discussion moderator's skill in balancing speaking times).

Other than that, if the methodology assumes that opinions form when points of view are shared among people who identify with each other (a premise that fits with Piaget's observation that development, whether cognitive or moral, occurs particularly in horizontal, peer relations), then relatively homogeneous groups are more appropriate for investigating the changing and rebuilding of opinions that come into conflict.

SUZANNE: Large social distances between participants in a group may make them hesitant to express their opinions. In

Canada, we noted that participation by 'native people', when we managed to involve them, was generally silent. In their traditional culture, it is the elders who call on the younger ones to speak. However, if we agree that the richness of dialogue and deliberation depends on a diversity of viewpoints in a democratic process, then it is also important for there to be heterogeneity in the group – possibly representative of the diversity in society. Of course there will be different points of view and conflicting opinions in heterogeneous groups. The basic rules of the Dialogues are proposed precisely so that young people can express different opinions and be heard, and so that they can hear different opinions and try to understand them.

GUSTAVO: There is no doubt that opting for diversity in the group make-up is decisive for the Dialogues' educational goal and is more realistic as regards their deliberative purposes. It seeks to reproduce the plurality of disputing values and viewpoints that characterizes our societies. In this case, however, the choice is made at an unavoidable cost to generalizing what is implicit in this (as in any) study. Diversity in the composition of the groups does not guarantee that the same diversity will be expressed in the final results, as suggested by the reports of participants keeping silent or of declarations made in the small groups, but suppressed in the plenaries.

NILTON: The Dialogues revealed the richness of dense listening which makes it possible, within the time constraints, for all and any kind of assertion, opinion or position to be explicitly stated. Democratic practice was produced by way of interaction and argumentation at two points. Firstly, in the small groups, young people had complete autonomy to speak more freely and informally, and also to prepare their posters and syntheses to take to the plenary. At a second point, in the plenaries, where the adult world was present, they employed argumentation and the 'art of persuasion' in order to build – multiple, not single – consensuses among all the groups.

LIVIA: The educational dimension brings a normative sense to the process: it aims to 'induce' young people somehow to engage in some action, to participate, according to a frame of reference which is interpreted through the facilitators' mediation. Once again, it seems to me that this normative dimension may introduce significant biases into the observation and knowledge dimension.

Certainly it is fundamental to have information in order to give qualified opinions and to have information and knowledge circulating is one important element in extending democracy. In that regard, we could say that participating in the Dialogues allows young people to acquire instruments for exercising citizenship. However, we cannot forget that in Brazilian society young people are considered much more in terms of negative attributes than positive ones. Their interventions in the public sphere are generally discredited by the adult world or, as Nilton says, are tutored, as if they were 'second-class citizens' who can only intervene through the mediation of adults. That is why the Dialogue process is an important space for experimenting with speaking, listening, and plural, horizontal dialogue.

SUZANNE: This happens in Canada as well. We asked organizations working with youth, a group of young people and a group of decision-makers for suggestions on how to change that situation. They offered advice – which we have taken – and gave interesting clues:

- It is important for the young people to have 'their space' and enough time to learn together, to gain confidence in their analyses and to develop concrete, ambitious, realistic proposals for change. Accordingly, we devoted a day and a half to the educational process, to deliberating and identifying both the actions that the young people would be willing to embrace and what they expect from institutions.

- It is useful to create 'another space', which is neither the space of adults nor the space of youth, but a 'third space' where both youth and adults discover a different way of relating, each respecting the other's world, which stimulates them to dialogue. We invited decision-makers who were interested and who were open to dialoguing with young people and they participated in two periods with the young people.

Three-day Dialogues are expensive and it is not easy to keep young people motivated all that time. We managed to do so because we had identified a lot of Dialogue themes in our focus groups with young people. We wanted to explore values, choices and roles in four public policy areas (education, work, environment and health). Many public and private institutions were interested in discovering young people's values and outlooks in these areas and were therefore willing to fund that effort. We had to work hard to get that funding and, in fact, it is a rare occurrence.

The important point I want to underline is that changing decision-makers' perceptions of young people and of their contribution, and changing young peoples' relationship with those responsible for policy decisions, takes time and requires favourable conditions.

GUSTAVO: Nonetheless, I believe the least impaired, or most favoured, dimension of the Dialogue process is the educational dimension. It is the immediate and subsequent effect that involvement in this kind of experience can have on the participants. In fact, it is a shame, as Suzanne says, that agencies do not usually fund subsequent process follow-up to systematically investigate how engaged Dialogue participants are in some form of participation.

LIVIA: Regarding the deliberative dimension, we were really quite worried about the possibility that the Dialogue would be experienced as yet another frustrating process, because we cannot guarantee that what was discussed and deliberated on will be heard and taken into consideration by government.

NILTON: We identified two possible repercussions of the Dialogue Days. On the one hand, certain young people may have 'made gains', in that they were listened to while they expressed their demands and proposals. If they expressed scepticism (or realism) in relation to future developments, it is worth including that element in our analyses by introducing the 'time' category. How in fact do you create a 'cultural melting pot' with regards to a public policy? On the other hand, the researchers and institutions involved in the study play a 'clear' mediation function in that the results are being socialized in a wide variety of forms.

GUSTAVO: To me the issue has two distinct, but interconnected components. The degree of frustration can be minimized if the young people are given a realistic assessment of how permeable institutions are to absorbing their deliberations at the outset. Another factor is the maturity necessary for them to understand that in political participation you don't always get or win what you want (which I suppose the method's educational component must contribute to, although not necessarily resolve). Among other things, the deliberations that may be constructed or predominate in one group's Dialogue may be different from the demands arising from the groups overall – or existing in society. Therefore, they are unlikely to be given priority, even in contexts where democratic policy-making processes prevail.

SUZANNE: I agree. The challenge is that we do not know how far the research results will be taken into consideration by responsible politicians. In the case of the Dialogues in Brazil, we knew that the Lula government's National Youth Secretariat was interested and that there was an opportunity to influence policies and programmes. We could guarantee the young people that their opinions would be aggregated in a report and that their voices would be heard by decision-makers. In Canada, we sent a copy of the report to all the participants together with a letter telling them who had been informed of the results and when. The young people could then be sure their voices were recorded and know that the organizers followed up on the work. We also told them clearly at the end of the Dialogues that they should keep tabs on decision-makers: democracy does not mean that whenever we give an opinion the authorities will act the way we want them to. In order for things to change, you have to engage, through whatever path you choose.

Without a doubt the Dialogues are an intervention in relation to complex political processes where various factors come into play. In both Brazil and Canada, civil-society organizations, collaborating with researchers, the media and others can play an important role in giving citizens a voice, creating conditions to influence decision-making processes and/or to broaden the reach of the dialogue in media networks and in communities. In Brazil, you have achieved a lot in that respect, and we can learn from you.

LIVIA: Without a doubt, Brazil has experimented with many different ways for citizens to intervene in political deliberations. The sectorial councils are one example and participatory budgets are another. Nonetheless, studies show that numerous stumbling blocks must be surmounted if these arrangements are really going to gain a significant role in the decision-making process. Politicians are rather unresponsive to electorate influence, which generally lacks legitimacy with the administrative 'machine'.

Along with that there is this whole rhetoric, which is definitely hegemonic in society, which holds people responsible for solving their problems. This accountability is expressed particularly strongly in relation to marginalized groups. Only by activating their own resources, 'rolling up their sleeves', as some of the young people said during the Dialogues, is it possible to improve the conditions of their lives and escape poverty. In that way, calls to participate have less to do with deliberation and decision-making than with engaging in some social activity to 'improve' the life conditions of the 'excluded'. 'Participation' has thus become rather ambiguous terrain where the political and social planes intermingle. Participating has become synonymous with implementing a service and deploying individual resources to benefit the community. Participation in the public sphere as a place for speaking out, for clashes among differing opinions, as a plural space where interests are negotiated with a view to taking the decisions that are intrinsic to collective living is therefore lost sight of. In that regard, we should remember Hannah Arendt's warnings about the need to separate social and political matters, as well as private and public spheres.

The Dialogues can represent spaces open to expressing and valuing differences of opinion, as well as public spaces for negotiating and constructing consensus. Confidence that everyone has the ability to give opinions and argue them in public seems to me to be at the root of the Dialogue proposal. Once again, it is worth remembering Hannah Arendt's thinking on social situations and the political conditions that prevent individuals from formulating and expressing opinions.

NILTON: Perhaps we should explore the relationship between public and private further and leave that contrast or ambiguity 'open', because it is what imbues the human condition. What is contradictory, (un)sayable, or forbidden is as present in moments of research as in young people's (and our own) daily lives. We are thinking about how what the young people say can be brought out 'explicitly', but in all its richness and complexity. That can perhaps help us understand the participatory 'process' in all of its countless possibilities which are not included in the more classic view (participation in the public sphere, in collective struggles, in claiming rights be granted etc.), but rather take place in mini-territories (school, family, neighbourhood, dance associations, music groups, churches, ecology and so on).

LIVIA: In my view, the Dialogue was more successful during the morning, when the young people were asked to discuss school, work, culture and leisure on the basis of their experiences since these are issues where they all have formed some opinion. In the afternoon, when the theme for discussion was participation, the exchange of opinions was less significant since the subject in most cases does not form part of their experience, is an abstract topic and, as we have seen, is full of ambiguities. Therefore it was difficult to make any interpretation in terms of the research data. Personally, I think that one important datum was discovering precisely that the young people do not consider 'participation' to be a significant theme that they think about. Rather, it is up to us researchers to interpret that datum in light of, among other things, the results of other studies on the subject.

GUSTAVO: This calls to mind what Bourdieu calls 'imposition of the problematic' in the provocative essay *Public opinion does not exist*. Even though in that case he is talking about public-opinion *surveys*, the problem that Livia has noted of abstracting themes in the middle of a Dialogue process is one example of how this issue can arise in qualitative research as well.

SUZANNE: Even though in Canada the discourse may be full of appeals to citizens to participate, government channels are generally quite guarded or even resistant to significant participation, unless they have encountered no major resistance to implementing a public policy (for instance, increased education costs or acceptance of nuclear energy) or if implementing their priorities requires citizens' engagement. In spite of this, there are 'model' decision-makers in various institutions who are influential and really interested in changing the paradigm and the practice on specific issues of importance to citizens. One has to identify and work with these people, with whoever has some influence and is willing to act. Without that, we run the risk of adding more cynicism to the 'fake' participation process.

LIVIA: On the one hand, the Dialogue was observed to 'produce a shift in the focus of [participants'] thinking, from private matters to public affairs, enabling them to express a critical analysis and an appreciation for collective action, and to situate themselves as subjects of thought and action (the Dialogue Day awakened them to the importance of thinking and taking a position with regard to the situation in Brazil').[4] On the other hand, it was said that 'young people tend to generically formulate participation (the path and the actions) for youth. There is a tendency for them not to see themselves as subjects of action on the path they choose, perhaps because they do not feel capable, in terms of real individual action, of actually intervening in real situations'.[5]

SUZANNE: How can they be made to feel responsible for acting both individually and collectively, and to see themselves as actors? That is one of the most important challenges in this deliberative process. It is relatively easy to identify what others (governments) should do. It is more difficult to acknowledge that, as a young citizen, I can make choices that I must live with: I can act or not, but how and with what consequences? The quality of the Manual and the group facilitation count for a lot, because it is necessary to stimulate their imaginations, elicit options and also deliberate on the personal choices and their consequences, and at the same to respect the participants. It is not easy. Do you have any ideas on that?

NILTON: It is possible to detect levels of participation and acceptance of responsibility in the Dialogues, both in minor matters and in larger ones. Examples of solidarity-based activities in education and health were extremely important in bringing young people to speak about their 'lived experience' in their countless, diverse situations. Perhaps 'stimulating the imagination' should start there. Especially in the small groups, we found young people looking for solutions to situations of that type. When they come to having to formulate policy more comprehensively, then it is up to the facilitators to act appropriately. In this way it may be possible to create conditions for young people to formulate creative proposals and not just grievances (blaming the adult world), both in the public/State sphere and in private matters.

LIVIA: Establishing subjects as actors is an important issue. What makes individuals feel concerned about a given issue and 'prevented' from acting and publicly taking a position? The factors that theories of social movements speak of include defending interests, the ability to envisage future scenarios and to choose rationally among possible alternatives, as well as the availability of material and symbolic resources. Under what conditions does collective action come about? How is it possible to stimulate individuals to become active subjects?

I would risk the hypothesis that, in Brazil today, young people are subjects of word and action, but of words and actions that take place in separate spaces (subordinate public spheres) which do not correspond to the normative definitions of the adult world. This 'speech' is expressed, for example, through music, dance and graffiti. Risk behaviours, such as drug use, may be considered moments of experimentation to nullify the separation between body and reason which is so characteristic of Western culture. Therefore these behaviours may express demands and a search for new meanings.

During the Dialogue, young people identify Path No. 3, which corresponds to youth groups mostly working in culture and communication, and which in fact attracts the most participants, as the 'fun' path. Does this identification of this path of action with no commitment, not reproduce the dominant discourse on what is considered legitimate participation for the 'good of the community'?

SUZANNE: I agree.

GUSTAVO: In cognitive social psychology, the theory of moral development put forward by Lawrence Kohlberg in the wake of a germinal study that the epistemologist Jean Piaget had published in 1933 (*The moral judgement of the child*), sustains that there is a development path running roughly from heteronomy to moral autonomy by way of three socio-moral points of view. These are the pre-conventional level, where individuals are concerned with their own interests and do not perceive the existence or importance of moral conventions and rules for living in society; the conventional level, where the individual's attitude is to maintain the social order and the *status quo*; and, finally, the post-conventional level, where – ideally – a critical perception of the historicity of moral norms and laws underpins a position of individual freedom with social responsibility, making it possible for autonomous subjects to emerge as potential agents of change of the present state of affairs.

Although this course is potentially open to everyone, the conditions and the sociocultural context of one's life are decisive factors in whether or not one advances through the stages. Frequent exposure to dialogue situations among peers facilitates genuine role-playing – the practice of putting oneself in someone else's place – and is therefore regarded as a strong driving force in the development of moral autonomy. From that standpoint, the Dialogue methodology is perfectly attuned to the educational goal of forming active citizens. However, practical experience with applying Kohlberg's theory in middle schools in the United States indicates that moral development occurs gradually over the course of months or years, which would suggest that participation in one or two Dialogue days would be insufficient to produce this type of maturation.

LIVIA: There's one last point I wanted to raise, returning to our opening remarks. Overlapping among the distinct functions of facilitator, animator and researcher led to many doubts among the people responsible for the Dialogues in Brazil. 'The posture of the facilitator and the team came to exert considerable influence over the young people's thinking. Although the purpose of the Dialogue (as mentioned many times since the invitation) has been to learn their opinions, on several occasions what one sees is that young people's expectations of the adults are very much mirrored in the teaching-learning relationship connected with their everyday interaction with teachers in the classroom'.[6]

SUZANNE: We also addressed that issue. What kind of relationship between the facilitator and the young people can work to favour dialogue? The young people we consulted before holding our Dialogues thought it was important for the small groups to be animated by young people. They also talked about some of the features necessary in plenary animators:

a) they should be perceived and acknowledged to be independent of government;

b) they should make the young people comfortable, in a horizontal relationship; and

c) they should make the young people see themselves in the issues raised, by using language that is not too academic and common expressions that young people also use, for example.

We opted to use co-animation where young adults take a leading role in the educational part and are accompanied by a professional animator in the large group. This assumes that the study has experienced animators available who can transit comfortably between the educational role, active listening and deliberative questioning.

LIVIA: The facilitators' experience is certainly an indispensable ingredient. Personally, I am in favour of regulating the profession of animator/facilitator. This would formalize their training and acknowledge the important role they play in many projects, both governmental and other, while also guaranteeing the quality of their work. Rather, the idea in Brazil is that anyone can be a 'facilitator', provided they intend to relate horizontally to the group. I believe, on the contrary, that it is a very important profession and therefore should be recognized and remunerated appropriately.

On the other hand, I think that Brazil has come a long way in using a variety of techniques to animate groups. These techniques go beyond words and involve the body, music, and body language. That is why I think that we could intervene more in the dynamics of the group, bringing in moments of play to help participants mesh and to optimize the time available for them to express themselves using a wide variety of registers.

SUZANNE: In our Dialogue with young people we include some group-animation techniques largely inspired by our exchanges on the subject. These include graphic animation, theatre, and music (percussion). We still have a lot to learn from you in this area.

NILTON: In Brazil, we have a tradition centring on the animator 'category' deriving from popular education which has its roots in the late 1950s and was strongly consolidated in the 60s. This was a time that converged strongly on the construction of a developmentalist national project. 'Cultural animators' became important, leading figures in the emancipation processes of the popular classes. Paulo Freire, who motivated many authors and social practices that advocate 'dialogue' as a source of methodological inspiration, reinforced the combination of 'the educational component, active listening and deliberative questioning' (*Learning to Question: A Pedagogy of Liberation*, Continuum 1989).

Regulating the profession of animator/facilitator may incur risks around the order of intensity of the engagement and, at the same time, of autonomy from ideological aspects. Its importance seems to me to lie in animator training that builds on a possible, harmonious combination of background life experience and theoretical and methodological training.

SUZANNE: Paulo Freire inspired the work of animators all over the world! The outlook and skills used in a Freire-based approach are powerful and represent a solid base for building a practice of dialogue. The Dialogue methodology that we adopted attempts to revive the rich tradition of dialogue, which has been forgotten in favour of ideological dispute and civic exclusion. It is evolving and I hope that this kind of conversation can enrich the practice in our countries.

Mediating between results and public policies

The concern over using the research results for public-policy purposes is of fundamental importance for this kind of survey, particularly because of its focus. Martins (1989) has already sounded this alert in his studies on social movements. In scientific research, he highlights the 'radical shift from the status of object to the status of objective'. He says: 'In intellectual production, that shift means emancipating the other from the status of object by emancipating ourselves, as intellectuals, from the status of tutors of knowledge' (p. 137).

From there, we can advance ideas about our 'role' in future developments. One of the contributions can be connected with the 'application' of research 'findings', by virtue of both the originality of the methodology used and the feedback that the young people gave us. However, we do not imagine that Brazil is currently open to this kind of interpretation and 'application' by those who formulate and 'execute' public policy at any level, federal, state or municipal. In any case, even if it were, this would not take the form of visible acknowledgement of documents forwarded by the institutions responsible for the research.

This text assumes the posture of a necessary mediating role between young people and public-policy makers. This is evident when we clearly state that the idea that youth is – permanently or temporarily – 'subdued' is a thing of the past. The study also resulted in interconnections in the adult world (among the survey formulators and our institutions) which proved highly beneficial, not just for us, but for the young people as well.

That said, we can claim to be producing a document that, by consolidating a field of knowledge on youth, affects both the academic/intellectual field and the political field. However in the latter case, the seats of public power are affected by the information in circulation rather then in a cause-and-effect manner.

Is that a limitation? We do not think so. Working with the notion of limits, of 'finitude', is also a learning process in knowledge production because this study is based on a situation that is very definitely circumscribed in time and place (seven metropolitan regions and the Federal District, during the year 2005), and on a limited number of participants.

We may perhaps be able to look for interactive situations where this collective paper can be discussed with public-policy makers and managers, taking inspiration from what Alberto Melucci says. 'You can adopt someone else's point of view only if you are aware of your own position in the field of social relations, discourses and languages. One additional detail: the other side of the dialogical option, in both civil and social life, is to be aware that you are working at the limit. That option has political consequences in that no single perspective can hope to play a totalizing role. Such a role can only be imposed by exerting force and violence directly' (Melucci 1994: 195).

We feel we have performed the task in part. We have tried to gather the viewpoint of the young people we surveyed, but without neglecting the conditions of our own status in the process. Another contribution is in the field of knowledge production on the subject of *Youth*. This contribution was made with a view to the goals stated at the start of this paper and giving prominence to the methodology used as a way of listening to (and, using the techniques implemented in the course of Dialogue Day, of recording) a sector of society that has much to say about its demands and its actions. That contribution is directed to the agencies, both within and outside the academic circuit, that shape young people, and to public and private agencies engaged in implementing actions targeting youth.

References

Abramo, Helena Wendel, *Cenas juvenis: punks e darks no espetáculo urbano*, Scritta (São Paulo, 1994).

Abad, José Miguel, 'Participación Juvenil y Políticas para su fomento: qué condiciones las determinan, tipos posibles y propuestas para mejorarla', mimeo. Paper presented to the seminar *Políticas Públicas de Juventud: un panel internacional*. (São Paulo, 2004).

Arendt, Hannah, *A condição humana*, 6th ed, Forense Universitária (Rio de Janeiro, 1993).

Bourdieu, Pierre, 'A opinião pública não existe', in Thiollent, Michel J. M., *Crítica metodológica, investigação social e enquete operária*. Coleção Teoria e História, vi, Editora Pólis (São Paulo, 1985).

Carrano, Paulo César, *Os jovens e a cidade: identidades e práticas culturais em Angra de tantos reis e rainhas*, Relume Dumará/Faperj (Rio de Janeiro, 2002).

Cloby, A. & Kohlberg. L., *The Measurement of Moral Judgment*, vols. i and ii. Cambridge University Press (Cambridge, 1987).

Costa, Ozanira Ferreira (Ed.) Relatório Sintético dos Grupos de Diálogo (CD-ROM), Research Project *Juventude Brasileira e Democracia: participação, esferas e políticas públicas*, Região Metropolitana de Brasília (2005).

Dayrell, Juarez, *A música entra em cena: o rap e o funk na socialização da juventude em Belo Horizonte*, Editora UFMG (Belo Horizonte, 2005).

Dayrell, Juarez (Ed.), Relatório dos Grupos de Diálogo da Região Metropolitana de Belo Horizonte (CD-ROM), Research Project *Juventude Brasileira e Democracia: participação, esferas e políticas públicas* (2005).

Fischer, Nilton Bueno (Ed.), Relatório qualitativo – Grupos de Diálogo da Região Metropolitana de Porto Alegre (CD-ROM). Research Project *Juventude Brasileira e Democracia: participação, esferas e políticas públicas* (2005).

Issacs, William, *Dialogue and the Art of Thinking Together*, Random House (New York, 1999).

Martins, José de Souza, *Caminhada no Chão da Noite: Emancipação política e libertação nos movimentos sociais do campo*, Hucitec (São Paulo, 1989).

Melucci, Alberto, Juventude, tempo e movimentos sociais, *Juventude e Contemporaneidade, Revista Brasileira de Educação*, v and vi, Anped (1997).

Melucci, Alberto, Movimentos Sociais, renovação cultural e o papel do conhecimento. Interview by Leonardo Avritzer & Timo Lyra, in Avritzer,

Leonardo (Ed.) *Sociedade civil e democratização*, pp. 183-211, Del Rey (Belo Horizonte, 1994).

Oliveira, Júlia Ribeiro de (Ed.), Relatório parcial dos Grupos de Diálogo da Região Metropolitana de Salvador (CD-ROM). Research Project *Juventude Brasileira e Democracia: participação, esferas e políticas públicas* (2005).

Piaget, J., *O Julgamento Moral na Criança*, (Orig. Ed. 1932), Mestre Jou (1977).

Power, F. C., Higgins Ann & Kohlberg, L., *Approach to Moral Education*, Columbia University (New York, 1989)

Reguillo, Rossana Cruz, *Emergencia de culturas juveniles: estrategias del desencanto*, Grupo Editorial Norma (Bogotá, 2000).

Rodrigues, Solange (Ed.), Relatório Síntese da Região Metropolitana de Rio de Janeiro (CD-ROM), Research Project *Juventude Brasileira e Democracia: participação, esferas e políticas públicas* (June 2005).

Serna, Leslie, 'Globalización y participación juvenil', *Revista de Estudios sobre Juventud-Jóvenes*. v/ii, July-Dec., Causa Joven (México, 1998).

Tommasi, Livia De (Ed.), Região Metropolitana do Recife (CD-ROM), Research Project *Juventude Brasileira e Democracia: participação, esferas e políticas públicas* (2005).

Yanekovich, Daniel, *The Magic of Dialogue: transforming conflict into cooperation*, Simon and Shuster (New York, 1999).

Chapter 5

DIALOGUE DAY
Young People's Opinions Formed in a Context of Research and Popular Education

*Solange dos Santos Rodrigues**

The research project *Brazilian Youth and Democracy: Participation, Spheres and Public Policies* was carried out in seven of Brazil's metropolitan regions and the Federal District, with young people from 15 to 24 years of age. It involved two methodological approaches: opinion polls of 8,000 young people and a qualitative study, which brought 913 youth together in Dialogue Groups in March and April, 2005.[1]

At the end of the Dialogue Day,[2] young participants were invited to answer two questions individually. One prompted them to send a message to decision-makers in Brazil. The other sought to record their assessment of the Dialogue Day.

This was an eagerly-awaited moment for the professionals conducting the survey, who had spent the day in the dual roles of dialogue facilitators and researchers. Now freed from the demanding task of facilitation, they could relax

---

* Solange dos Santos Rodrigues is a sociologist and researcher with the NGO Iser Assessoria – www.iserassessoria.org.br, and Project Supervisor, *Juventude Brasileira e Democracia – participação, esferas e políticas públicas* for the Rio de Janeiro metropolitan region.

and listen to the young people's opinions of the experience they had just had. They were asked to answer the following question: 'Of all that happened here today, what was most important?'.

Although the question was formulated in such a way as to direct answers towards positive aspects,[3] it did nonetheless suggest an *evaluation* of the Day, without actually using the term. This strategy proved worthwhile, because these interviewees tend to associate 'evaluation' with measurement of their performance at school, generally expressed in terms of quantitative marks or grades.

The way the question was phrased prompted them to qualify their answers, and to give content to their evaluation. In addition, the question was open enough to allow them to freely address any aspect of the Dialogue Day. We were particularly curious to hear what they would say. Their answers often surprised and moved us and gave us a wealth of material for later analysis.[4]

This paper analyzes the young people's opinions on Dialogue Day and examines the methodological path chosen. It reveals that what took place was a learning process for both young participants and researchers, thereby situating this study in the field of popular education and social intervention.

Young people evaluate Dialogue Day

The young people from various regions of Brazil gave very similar opinions basically related to four themes. The first set comprises answers that see the Dialogue Groups as places where they *would get their chance to speak to the group*. These answers emphasize the opportunity to express their opinions which led to an interchange. They valued the fact that their ideas were listened to and taken into consideration.

Another set of answers relates to the field of *sociability*. Young people stressed the importance of having the opportunity to meet new people, extend networks of social relations and to perceive a shared identity.

The third set of answers talks about the *learning* process set in motion during the Dialogue Day. The young people valued various aspects such as the content, form and repercussions of those learnings.

The young people also emphasized that the Dialogue Groups afforded them an opportunity to *think about Brazil*, its problems and the ways to surmount them. In this round of evaluation, there were also young participants who took the opportunity to say that they had enjoyed the experience and were grateful for having been invited to take part in the study.

Young people speak out

> 'What was most important was that I could express myself, because I'm very shy.' (Rio de Janeiro)[5]

> 'I liked this opportunity we had to put forward our opinions, discuss things that I don't think I would ever discuss otherwise.' (Belo Horizonte)

> 'I had never taken part in a debate that gave young people their own active voice. I am grateful for having participated.' (Salvador)

> 'It was really good. I never thought we'd have the chance to say what we think and feel.' (Porto Alegre)

> '(...) generally, when they call young people in to hear a talk, they talk about drugs, contraceptives, all those things we already know about, and this one didn't; it was different because we gave our opinions; that was great.' (São Paulo)

As can be seen from the quotes, the young people spoke their minds on Dialogue Day. What is expressed is both individual and collective. It was an opportunity to overcome shyness, to disclose opinions and feelings, and to have an active voice. It was an important moment because they were stimulated to talk about matters they are not usually consulted on. They expressed ideas, thoughts and feelings that only gain their full meaning when there is someone prepared to listen to them. The Dialogue Groups were also an opportunity to exercise listening skills:

> 'The most important thing that happened today was hearing different points of view, hearing what other young people want and, mainly, hearing what life is like for each one here, their life histories, which are so different from mine. To me personally, that was very important.' (Rio de Janeiro)

The chosen methodological path allowed young people to consider different opinions and exchange experiences with other people coming from a variety of places and social situations. Talking and listening are constituent elements of the *dialogue* process that comprise a category that covers many of the answers. In the Dialogue Groups, the young people perceived that 'coexistence is going to call for concessions, tolerance, respect for diversity and difference'.[6] It was also interesting to note that there were young participants who, in their evaluations, referred to the commitments made at the start of the Dialogue Day:[7]

> 'What was important about what happened today is that I learned to listen without criticizing (...) Here we had to learn to listen and be quiet, and then to speak out at the right moment.' (São Paulo)

> 'Well, I thought today was important because it was a meeting of people with different opinions, that nonetheless should all be respected.' (Rio de Janeiro)

We were surprised by one boy who declared that the most important thing was 'taking part in a conversation among young people', which was an unprecedented experience for him. We know that young people talk among themselves in the various contexts where they socialize – at school or at work, in their neighbourhood, their circle of friends and leisure activities. Perhaps the novelty lay in the kind of conversation, in the situation created especially for the purpose in the context of a survey, where they were interacting with other people they had just met, all coming from different places and with differing life histories.

So these were a different kind of dialogue, where they could see and experience confrontation among conflicting ideas, but where diverging opinions were respected. Or, as one boy put it, 'with no fights or arguments'.

> 'It was the interaction of so many different thoughts (...) everyone expressing their point of view, their way of thinking and everyone joining in a healthy, friendly dialogue.' (Salvador)

> 'To me the most important thing that happened was learning to dialogue with people from different classes, different kinds of people, right? People are opinionated and we have to put up with each other.' (Belém)

> 'What I got out of today here – and I think that goes for everyone – is that everyone's got their own opinion, everyone's got a different opinion and we can talk about that.' (Rio de Janeiro)

> 'What I think is really interesting was the sharing. Everyone spoke, we all agreed or disagreed, but even so everyone was open to other people's opinions and changed their opinions.' (Recife)

They recognized the importance of working as a group to produce a synthesis: 'if we [each] analyzed it all on our own, we wouldn't come to the same conclusion' (Brasília). This shows that some young people learned the fundamental principles of the methodology by which in order for opinion to be formed, there has to be access to information and dialogue about that information. This dialogue may then alter or reinforce the participants' initial ideas:

> 'I think the day was productive, because I even changed my opinion on some points. That's what's good about debate: you don't just stick with

the same opinion, you see everyone's opinions and take in whatever's best.' (São Paulo)

'I had an opinion when I arrived that was totally different from the one I am leaving with.' (Belo Horizonte)

'I liked the freedom of expression, how the dialogue was so full and varied. I think that everyone here is going to leave with a different idea or else with their ideas strengthened.' (Recife)

This interchange of ideas was also seen as a mechanism that produced learning, which will be considered in more detail below. It should be said, however, that the young participants saw the interchange as extending beyond the relationship established among themselves, to include the researchers/facilitators, the institutions that promoted the survey and the government agencies which were going to receive the results. Some young participants said the most important thing about the day was to see that there are people and institutions interested in hearing, recording and considering their opinions:

'I liked knowing that there are people who concern themselves with young people because generally people impose what they think is best for us, without getting our opinion.' (Rio de Janeiro)

'Most important is that today I argued and was recorded. Because I always argue and argue but nobody listens to us... And now "they"[8] are going to listen, they're going to have to listen to our opinion.' (Rio de Janeiro)

'To me the most important thing that happened was seeing the government and other institutions take this initiative, and seeing that there are people – who aren't young people – concerned to hear our opinion. And they're not imposing opinions, but giving us the opportunity to develop our own ideas.' (Rio de Janeiro)

As pointed out by the researchers in Porto Alegre, this collection of declarations speaks of 'a recognition that is so necessary to young people, that here is someone who has something to say and who places a high value on the right to be heard'.[9] Generally, however, the same declarations suggest that young people's opinions are not considered. To what extent are they encouraged to express their ideas and opinions freely in the social spaces where they get their experience of daily life – family, school, work, and the groups and organizations they take part in? Do these promote attentive, respectful listening? Do they make true interchange possible? Do they take young people's knowledge, concerns and wishes into consideration?[10] That lacuna may explain why young people are surprised that there are people, institutions and government agencies ready to listen to them and take their demands into account. And they are grateful for the opportunity.

The first core group of themes highlighted by the young people when they were asked to say the most important thing that happened on the Dialogue Day can be summarized by saying 'Words given centre stage'. This group includes the opportunity for youth to voice their own words, listen to others, exchange and reformulate ideas and conceptions, and to perceive that there is an interest in recording their opinions.

Young people extend their social networks

The Dialogue Group participants pointed to the importance of having experienced other dimensions of living together in society, by meeting new people and discovering identities. This was one type of response that appeared in all of the metropolitan regions surveyed. In Brasília, for instance: 'I was very happy to meet the gang' or in São Paulo, 'I liked making friends with everyone I met here, that was great'.

Particularly the young people living in the two largest metropolitan regions, São Paulo and Rio de Janeiro, felt that what was important was that they had gone beyond their immediate circle – their neighbourhood, municipality and the places where they spend their free time – and crossed the metropolis to meet people who, in turn, had come from other places. It shows they are living in times when people do not circulate very much in the cities, limiting their opportunities to share experiences.

At the start of the Dialogue Days (before the small group work), some young participants were rather shy and had difficulty fitting in, but by the end of the day they were participating in animated conversations, and swapping addresses and phone numbers. Many left in groups, extending their time together until the moment came when they would have to catch transport home to their own neighbourhoods.

Participating in the Dialogue Groups also enabled them to penetrate social spaces unfamiliar to most of them, such as universities, NGO offices, clubs and hotels. The entire experience allowed them to expand their networks of social activities and social relations, and also to extend their knowledge of the metropolis, both physically and symbolically.

This encounter between individuals experiencing their youth in Brazil's metropolitan areas during same period of the early 21st century made it evident to some of the young people that they shared ideas, problems, aspirations and plans:

> 'I also thought it interesting because all of a sudden you're meeting young people from different backgrounds, with different ideas, but with a lot of things in common that can improve.' (Porto Alegre)

> 'There are people here that I've never seen before in my life, who live a really long way from me, and who have the same opinion as me. It's important to know that. And that they want a better country. Both me and other people who I saw here today.' (Rio de Janeiro)

Therefore one of the immediate results of the Dialogue Groups was that some discovered a common *identity*. Even when living a long way from one another, they realized that they faced similar problems and lived under similar conditions. This dimension, the recognition of a common identity, was also signalled by the team of researchers in Recife.[11]

However, they also perceived the differences that mark their diverse social backgrounds.[12] They recognized that, at times, they had different points of view but, by dialoguing they were able to discover affinities and to see that they shared ideas and wanted a better future for Brazil.[13]

Young people learn through the Dialogue Groups

A significant portion of the participants highlighted the learning dimension as the most important aspect of Dialogue Day, saying that they had been given the opportunity to *learn*. While some answers were generic ('To me the most important thing that happened was that I was able to broaden my knowledge.' – Rio de Janeiro), there were also answers that specified just what had been learned:

> 'I learned a lot, it was better than a public school. I learned about politics and society.' (Brasília)

> 'I learned the "pros and cons" line of reasoning, because you can't think just about your own opinion, you have to consider the pros and the cons.' (Rio de Janeiro)

> 'One of the lessons I learned here is that young people today aren't empty. There's a lot in these young heads. What's lacking is for us to really fight for these goals (...)' (Recife)

This kind of learning may mean going deeper into certain subjects ('politics and society', in the example quoted), but it may also translate into a different way of looking at certain issues ('consider the pros and cons')[14] or may represent a shift in hard and fast opinions ('young people today aren't empty'). Some participants also stressed learnings intimately bound to the subject of the research and the Dialogue methodology:

> 'I learned that we shouldn't just wait for governments, but that there are things *we* can do ourselves.' (Salvador)

> 'My opinion used to be that volunteer work and the group were enough on their own, but then you could also see that without politics it's difficult.' (Belo Horizonte)

The first quote shows that some young participants understood it was not enough to abstractly discuss the options offered during the Dialogue Day. They realized that this thinking exercise involved citizens' assuming some personal engagement in whatever course was chosen. The second quote indicates that an initial choice was upgraded through the incorporation of constituent elements from other proposals under consideration. In this specific case, the young person discovered that approaches being presented as separate options (acting as an individual or with a group and acting through institutional politics) may at first seem mutually exclusive, but in fact are complementary.

Also in regards to the methodology, the researchers of the Salvador metropolitan region drew attention to the emphasis that the young people placed on the distinction between 'dispute' and 'dialogue', and their satisfaction 'with the proposal to look for similarities in small groups and later with all the participants in the Dialogue Group'.[15]

It is important that several young people underlined the way this learning came about. It has already been shown above how highly they valued the interchange of ideas that took place on Dialogue Day. Here, the emphasis is on the role that interchange played in the learning process:

> 'To me the most important thing that happened was to see us educating ourselves, each other, listening to one another.' (São Paulo)

The dominant pattern in young people's experience is to learn from adults, from people of other generations (parents and teachers). The novelty to the young people was in the perception that it was possible to learn from other young people.

In the same vein, there were young people who referred to learning about the process of interchange:

> 'We learned to dialogue, just a little, but we learned. We learned to listen to other people's proposals. (...) My opinion fits with yours, or yours complements mine.' (Belém)

> 'We learned from one another, didn't we? To respect each other's space, to listen to each other...' (Rio de Janeiro)

They learned to deal with differing opinions and even to reconsider their own initial opinions on the basis of what they heard. Some young people emphasized having learned about what are considered basic, constructive elements of social living, supposedly shared by everyone. For example, 'The important thing I learned here was to work in a group.' (Belo Horizonte). And, 'I learned to debate and to coexist with other people.' (Rio de Janeiro).

This learning grew out of practice and was experienced through the interchange of ideas rather than just by receiving abstract concepts. In this way it came to constitute an incorporated value that might be activated in other situations.

Also worth noting is that, when they recognized the Dialogue Day as a learning experience, they immediately drew comparisons with the teaching-learning processes that go on in school. There is a quote above from a boy in Brasília who singles out his learning that day about politics and society, and says it was 'better than a public school'. Another boy from the same metropolitan region said that the subject discussed in the survey 'is not explored at our school'. Another one, from the Porto Alegre metropolitan region, said that 'at school I was afraid to give an opinion in case it was wrong, but there was none of that here'.

This leads us to a series of questions about the education that goes on in schools, its content and methodologies, and about the relationships between the educators and those they are educating. This is especially important in the of a knowledge society, where so much information is available but does not automatically lead to understanding our realities.

What is the role of educators in selecting, ordering and offering information for young people to think about, so that it can be re-elaborated and lead to new knowledge? A clue can be found in one young girl's willingness to radiate the experience gained in the Dialogue Day:

> 'I intend to pass all of this on at my school, to organize a group to discuss these things, just like we did here, because the people at my school need this.' (Rio de Janeiro)

Another very significant dimension in this set of learnings is that the Dialogue Day made the young people think, and brought out knowledge they already held without being aware of it:

> 'In fact, I didn't even know that I had any knowledge about this subject, and I spoke quite a lot here today, and I learned even more from you others too. I learned from myself. I just needed someone to motivate me.' (Belém)

In the final round of remarks, where the young people could talk about whatever they wanted, some took the opportunity to speak about various aspects of the Dialogue experience:

> 'I left home thinking that it would be something else. I learned what dialogue is. It's really good to discuss issues facing Brazil, it's important to lay out what you think, how things can change.' (Brasília)

In this brief comment, the boy demonstrated that he was surprised by the methodological proposal, remarked on the importance of having room to express ideas, recognized how he had learned, and valorized the opportunity to discuss the situation in Brazil and the possibilities of social change. This leads us into another dimension of the Dialogue Day which was emphasized by some of the young people.

Young people thinking about Brazil

For young people, verbal self-expression, meeting and learning are valuable in themselves. In addition, some young participants said that the most important thing about the day was having thought about what is happening in Brazil:

> 'Today I thought the day was important because of the thinking it prompted, because sometimes you're so busy working and studying that you end up forgetting the real situation in the country.' (São Paulo)

> 'The most important thing that happened here is that I learned about a lot of problems that affect Brazil and I didn't know.' (Rio de Janeiro)

In this way, by focussing on youth relations, democracy and participation in the public sphere, the Dialogue Day provided an opportunity *to find out about the situation in Brazil and think about it.*[16] This is not just thinking for its own sake. There were young people who emphasized that the discussions spurred them to look for alternatives in order to change real situations:

> 'Every one of us left with a wealth of new ideas, of possible ways of changing ourselves and the country we live in.' (Salvador)

> 'Well, to me the most important thing that happened here today was participating in this meeting, knowing that everyone here has different ideas for changing Brazil, for how to be able to change the situation we live in. And to me that was very significant.' (Rio de Janeiro)

> 'What I most liked was hearing other people's ideas, but with the same purpose of looking for a solution to the problems there are in Brazil, which in my opinion are extremely serious.' (Porto Alegre)

Others pointed to the link between thought and action:

'I'm anxious to get back to my city and do something to try to change. We're not going to forget this. So many ideas were put forward here. So it shouldn't be just a study, but a programme that perceives how young people are situated in society.' (Porto Alegre)

'This type of meeting is an encouragement for us to go right out and start taking action.' (Salvador)

'I believe that from today on, all of us here, this select group, are going to change how we act out there, how we act in society.' (Rio de Janeiro)

When invited to talk about their lives in this way, as Brazilians, there were some youth who pointed out that the Dialogue Day allowed them to broaden the focus and examine the situation in the country, and they referred particularly to the need to bring about changes. The result was that the focus of the thinking shifted from private concerns to public affairs. This created opportunities to express critical analysis and to valorize collective action through thinking and acting people.

On the other hand, in the course of the Dialogue Day, young participants clearly expressed the difficulties of participating in the public sphere. These had to do both with the context of extreme social inequalities that restrict rights and with the lack, inadequacy or inaccessibility of existing spaces for social participation.

One of the study's major conclusions is that in order to leverage effective youth participation and thereby strengthen democracy, social movements, youth and other civil society organizations and the State will have to make determined efforts to put listening mechanisms in place. This will help valorize youth's immediate interests and encourage their active citizenship.

Dialogics and learning, research and popular education

The young participants' assessment of the survey shows that the experience was basically perceived as a process of education through dialogue. In the free session at the end of the Day, young participants made a point of stressing that they had been able to express their opinions, to dialogue and to learn. In all the metropolitan regions, around 40 per cent mentioned the interchange of ideas, and another 40 per cent learning, while some linked the two dimensions, saying they had learned through the dialogue.

The young participants recognized the logic of dialogue (dialogics) that governed this research. That logic generated interlocution on several different levels – among young people, between them and the researchers, among researchers, and among NGOs, government and society. It is evident that 'the dialogue was not just a method, but that it also stood as a principle'[17] producing collective learning. The link between dialogue and learning is constitutive of this chosen methodological path:

> 'Better still if, in this investigative process, it were possible to engage these young people in an exercise that would strengthen the democratic principles investigated, and make for shared, thoughtful learning by young participants and researchers'.[18]

Through the dialogue, the young people were really able to think about the problems affecting Brazilian youth, systematize their demands, consider different alternative ways of participating in the public sphere to satisfy those demands and formulate proposals. In short, they experienced a kind of participation that may lead to them valorizing and learning about democracy.

There is another more immediate level, however, where the methodology sets out to produce learning:

'The *Choice Work Dialogue* methodology also considers the investigative process as a learning process where the participants have the opportunity to access information, make connections between facts and circumstances, perceive conflicts and engage in a collective process where it is possible to learn how far opinions change when people have access to information and then dialogue on a given subject'.[19]

One of the challenges facing the team responsible for this kind of study is to guarantee the participants official information. This explains the extreme care taken in the preparation of the instruments used in the dialogue. The Workbook (the template for the dialogue in the study) was the product of rigorous research, the content of which had to be presented in an accessible form to young people that could be taken home when the work was done; the summary of the main ideas was attractively set out with sounds and graphics in a presentation projected on a large screen; and the venue was hung with banners.

Therefore, researchers were aware of the educational dimension to the study and its methodology. In addition, most of them are also involved in training activities of some kind, either as university professors or as specialists in NGOs working with capacity-building and strengthening citizenship. However, during the Dialogues, we had to be careful to relegate the educator's role to the background and act as facilitators of the youth dialogue and as researchers observing the process of opinion formation.

That is why it is no surprise to hear the participants say that the most important thing about the day was the interchange of ideas – giving their opinion, hearing others, considering, reinforcing or changing opinions, and arriving at syntheses. However, the emphasis they placed on the learning process did surprise us. One imagines that the young people themselves were surprised: they gained access to a variety of knowledge in a social situation where it was not expected since what they had been invited to was nothing like a class, course or talk.

This learning dimension was very conspicuous, to the point that on several occassions participants reformulated the question that had been proposed to them and written on a poster in front of them. Instead of answering 'What was most important about what *happened* here today?', many of them started off by saying 'The most important thing I *learned* here today was …'. Sometimes, we facilitators reminded them of the original question, but the young people went on talking about learnings.

For these reasons, the emphasis they placed on learning, the explicit references to this dimension of the investigative process, can be considered as an *unforeseen result* of the study. Something similar is described in numerous other studies, where subjects invited to respond to questions in a questionnaire or interview declare that the experience led to unexpected learning because it made them ponder the realities of their lives and become aware of certain processes and challenges. This may have significant repercussions in terms of momentum for action. This happened in the Dialogue Groups as well.

Lastly, it is important to underline the potential influence of the institutional framework in which this study was carried out. The study was proposed by two leading Brazilian NGOs– Ibase and Pólis – which along with other civil society organizations work to improve democracy and overcome the profound social inequalities characteristic of Brazilian society. The survey was performed by a network of NGOs (mostly) and universities.

'Using a method that allies principles of academic research and of popular education, while remaining distinct from both of them'[20] was a challenge, but I think that the methodology is really quite appropriate to the task of knowledge production as performed in the NGO sphere. Generally speaking, research conducted by NGOs is designed to give a qualified response to demands brought by social movements and/or it is intended to be effective in influencing social processes and conflicts.

One of the factors responsible for the success of this undertaking was the interrelationship between researchers from NGOs whose activities are shaped by the principles of popular education and which advocate for youth rights. These include Ação Educativa (São Paulo), Cria (Salvador), Equip and Redes e Juventudes (Recife), Inesc (Brasília), Iser Assessoria (Rio de Janeiro) and Unipop (Belém) – and academic scholars who valorize the work of university extension – from federal universities in Minas Gerais (UFMG, Belo Horizonte), Rio Grande do Sul (UFRGS) and Rio de Janeiro (UFF).

One of the principles of popular education is learning from practice. There is no doubt that the organizations and researchers that participated in this thinking exercise had the opportunity to bring their own forms of social intervention into dialogue with knowledge produced during the study. This is conducive to acquiring new learnings and fits well with the chosen methodological path. As mentioned above, it seeks to foster 'shared, thoughtful learning by the young participants and researchers'.

Another principle of popular education is the inseparable relationship between knowledge and action. Perceiving that there were young people who were stimulated to think about their lives and their country and to take a position was one of the most significant fruits of this investigative process. There were even participants who showed a willingness to engage in the forms of social action being examined during the Day.

We were glad that these young people's participation in the study may have short- and long-term repercussions on their activities in society. The thinker Paulo Freire invites us to perceive in the educational process that 'the given world is a world giving of itself and, for that very reason, can be changed, transformed, reinvented'.[21] According to Freire, in this way, 'the viewpoint of the learning changes'.[22] This is true not just for the young people, but also for the researchers and organizations involved in this study, which can be changed and transformed.

The work done on Dialogue Day revealed another principle of the relationship established between individuals in a popular education process: commitment. As one boy put it, the study was being carried out by people and institutions with a commitment to youth:

> 'It's great to know there are people concerned about the young, who fight for our rights, who are concerned for us, who are on our side.' (Rio de Janeiro)

This declaration not only surprised our region's research team, it moved us. It was encouragement to reassert our commitment to ensuring effective rights for the young people of our country. We were researchers, educators and citizens and the multiple nature of our work was explicit.

To summarize, the Dialogue Groups research methodology offered the young participants a singular opportunity to work in groups. It allowed them to express their opinions, listen to others, debate ideas, seek syntheses so as to formulate proposals – in short, to collectively construct knowledge. They were also able to argue their propositions in a larger group and had to produce arguments to do so. In doing so, they learned in a variety of ways and situated the set of problems they were examining – youth demands and participation – in the broader context of the contradictions that mark Brazilian society. That is to say that the debate on one subject contributed to forming these young people and gained an educational dimension, bringing it close to many of the principles of popular education. This education is taking place outside the school classroom –

which, notwithstanding, could incorporate these methodological principles into the formal education process.

Meanwhile, the perception that various agents and institutions took an interest in their ideas gave a sense of visibility to the young people, most of whom are poor and whose rights are continuously abused. While one of the goals was to 'engage these young people in an exercise that would strengthen the democratic principles being investigated', another purpose of this study carried out among NGOs was to have political impact and to contribute to broadening the rights of Brazilian youth. The intention of this much broader goal is to ensure that government policies are truly public and to surmount the yawning social and economic inequalities that mar Brazilian society.

References

Freire, Paulo, *Educação na cidade*, Cortez (São Paulo, 1991).

Research Reports

Corti, Ana Paula, Souza, Raquel & Oliveira, Elisabete, *Relatório da Etapa Qualitativa (Grupos de Diálogo). Região Metropolitana de São Paulo*. Research Project *Juventude Brasileira e Democracia: participação, esferas e políticas públicas*, Ação Educativa, Ibase, Pólis (São Paulo, June 2005).

Costa, Ozanira Ferreira da, Figueiredo, Karina & Ribeiro, Perla, *Relatório dos Grupos de Diálogo. Região Metropolitana de Brasília. Que Brasil queremos? E como chegar lá?*, Inesc, Ibase, Pólis (Brasilia, June 2005).

Dayrell, Juarez, Leâo, Geraldo & Gomes, Nilma Lino, *Relatório Preliminar dos Grupos de Diálogo. Região Metropolitana de Belo Horizonte*. Research Project *Juventude Brasileira e Democracia: participação, esferas e políticas públicas*, Observatório da Juventude da UFMG, Ibase, Pólis (Belo Horizonte, June 2005).

De Tommasi, Lívia, Brandâo, Marcílio & Braga, Graça Elenice, *Relatório Região Metropolitana do Recife*, Research Project *Juventude Brasileira e Democracia: participação, esferas e políticas públicas*, Equip, Ibase, Pólis (Recife, 2005).

Fischer, Nilton Bueno, Souza, Carmem Zeli, Ramos, Nara, Stecanela, Nilda & Salva, Sueli, *Relatório Qualitativo dos Grupos de Diálogo. Região Metropolitana de Porto Alegre*. Research Project *Juventude Brasileira e Democracia: participação, esferas e políticas públicas*, PPGEDU/UFRGS, Ibase, Pólis (Porto Alegre, June 2005).

Ibase & Pólis, 'A metodologia dos Grupos de Diálogo', in Research Project *Juventude Brasileira e Democracia: participação, esferas e políticas públicas*. Relatório Global (CD-ROM), Ibase, Pólis (Rio de Janeiro, January 2006).

Oliveira, Júlia Ribeiro, Silva, Ana Paula Carvalho & Colaço, Fernanda, *Relatório Parcial dos Grupos de Diálogos. Região Metropolitana de Salvador*. Research Project *Juventude Brasileira e Democracia: participação, esferas e políticas públicas*, Cria, Ibase, Pólis (Salvador, 2005).

Ribeiro, Eliane, Lânes, Patrícia & Carrano, Paulo, Research Project *Juventude Brasileira e Democracia: participação, esferas e políticas públicas*, Relatório Final, Ibase, Pólis (Rio de Janeiro, November 2005).

Rodrigues, Solange, Cunha, Marilena & Aguiar, Alexandre, *Relatório Qualitativo - Grupos de Diálogo. Região Metropolitana do Rio de Janeiro*. Research Project *Juventude Brasileira e Democracia: participação, esferas e políticas públicas*, Iser Assessoria/Observatório Jovem da UFF, Ibase, Pólis (Rio de Janeiro, June 2005).

Silva, Lúcia Isabel da Conceição, Viana, Rosely Risuenho & Silva, Francisca Guiomar da, *Relatório Qualitativo, Região Metropolitana de Belém*. Research Project *Juventude Brasileira e Democracia: participação, esferas e políticas públicas*, Unipop, Ibase, Pólis (Belém, 2005).

Chapter 6

BRAZIL AND CANADA
Learning through Collaboration

*Mary Pat MacKinnon**
Suzanne Taschereau

This chapter chronicles the story and results of a rich collaboration between several NGO and research partners (Ibase, Pólis, Canadian Policy Research Networks and IDRC) that spanned design, implementation, analysis and reporting of an innovative and ambitious project: the Brazilian youth and democracy dialogue. Motivated by a shared commitment to strengthen democracies through the meaningful engagement of young people, the partners contributed their knowledge, experiences and passion to produce a credible process and product. Recounting the key milestones and elements of this collaboration, the authors explore the challenges addressed, identify factors that contributed to the project's success, share learnings and reflect on what is needed to advance the theory and practice of public dialogue (with particular reference to young people)

---

* About the authors:
Mary Pat MacKinnon and Suzanne Taschereau are project advisors to the Brazilian youth and democracy dialogue initiative.

in Canada and Brazil. The chapter concludes by identifying particular themes that require focused attention to help improve and sharpen methods, results and impacts of deliberative dialogue.

> '... dialogue is a kind of necessary posture to the extent that humans have become more and more critically communicative beings. Dialogue is a moment where humans meet to reflect on their reality as they make and remake it.'
>
> Paulo Freire[1]

> 'Some may think that to affirm dialogue – the encounter of men and women in the world in order to transform the world – is naively and subjectively idealistic. There is nothing, however, more real or concrete than people in the world, than humans with other humans.'
>
> Paulo Freire[2]

Introduction

Over the last several years, a group of Brazilian and Canadian researchers have constructed a solid bridge across North and South America to share and enlarge collective understanding and knowledge about why and how to engage young people in their respective democracies. Reflecting the authors' perspectives as Canadian researchers and practitioners, this article tells the story of this international partnership. It recounts key milestones and elements of the collaboration, explores the challenges encountered, shares learnings and reflects on what is needed to advance cross cultural research relationships. It also identifies areas warranting closer scrutiny, including improving deliberative dialogue methods and assessing the results and impacts of deliberative dialogue practice and research, with a particular focus on engaging young people in democracy.

Context, impetus and milestones

The International Development Research Centre (IDRC) – a Canadian publicly funded arms-length research organization – provided the inspiration for the creation of this international project. Without IDRC's financial support, intellectual curiosity and active involvement, this partnership would not have materialized. The partners in this endeavour were IDRC, Instituto Brasileiro de Análises Sociais e Economicas (Ibase), Instituto de Estudos de Formacão e Assessoria em Politicas Sociais (Pólis) and Canadian Policy Research Networks (CPRN).

IDRC was one of several funders of a national citizens' dialogue on Canada's future[3] undertaken by CPRN (2002-03) in partnership with Viewpoint Learning Inc. Intrigued by the methodology and results, IDRC, led by Federico Burone (IDRC Director for Latin America and Caribbean Region), saw the potential for its adaptation to South America and Brazil in particular where the newly elected Labour government led by President Lula had flagged youth disengagement as a societal challenge demanding attention. Burone organized a workshop in Brasilia in early October 2003 (*Citizens' Dialogue: Opportunities, Methodology and Lessons Learned*) at which CPRN's Director of Public Involvement, Mary Pat MacKinnon, presented the results of and lessons from CPRN's dialogue on Canada's future. Other presenters included the heads of Ibase and Pólis (Candido Gryzbowski and Silvio Caccia Bava), Cezar Alvarez (representing President Lula's newly elected office), as well as other government officials and academics from Latin America.

Subsequent meetings and discussions with the President's office involving Ibase, Pólis, IDRC and CPRN led to the launch (halfway through 2004) of an ambitious and innovative research dialogue project called *Brazilian Youth and Democracy: participation, spheres and public policies*. The selection of youth and democracy as the dialogue theme reflected a collective growing disquietude shared by civil society and government about the disconnection between youth and democratic participation and the failure of democratic institutions to adapt democratic practices to better engage youth. The dialogue project had two key action-oriented policy objectives:

1. to provide evidence on how young people from metropolitan areas in Brazil assess the current need and opportunities for their social integration and what they expect for the future of the country with regard to poverty, basic social services, labour markets, market niches and expectations for their lives; and

2. to facilitate the use of research-based outcomes in local, provincial and national discussions to influence on-going youth public policy design and implementation processes.

Concurrent with the development of the Brazil project, CPRN was embarking on its own investigation motivated by a similar concern about youth participation in democracy - by midway through 2004 this had become an important research theme for the organization.[4] Shortly after, CPRN had launched its own initiative: the *National Dialogue and Summit on Engaging Young Canadians*. CPRN's youth dialogue project had several objectives:

- to understand how young people define active citizenship;

- to learn about what would motivate young people to become more engaged in public life;

- to identify what needs to change within public, community and private institutions to encourage more active citizenship; and

- to learn about young people's hopes and expectations for themselves and for others and the values that underpin their vision for Canada.

Thus, when IDRC approached CPRN to provide its partner, Ibase and Pólis with training, technical assistance and support[5] during the preparation, implementation and reporting phases, we were quick to sign on. This alignment of interest, timing and resources proved to be very productive for the Canadian and Brazilian collaboration.

Before sketching key milestones that describe the collaboration's evolution, a note on the philosophy and approach that shaped the relationships among the Brazil project team, IDRC and CPRN may be helpful. CPRN approached and participated in this project guided by the belief that it had at least as much, if not more, to learn as to contribute. Rather than seeing the partnership as one of simply transferring methodology from Canada to Brazil, team members envisioned working together to define what was needed. The relationship was entered into with all parties aware of the complexity of the initiative, understanding that cross cultural collaboration required respect and openness, and recognizing that it would certainly demand flexibility and acceptance of uncertainties and unpredictable outcomes.

Table 1: Collaboration Milestones

August – September 2004:
Initial Exchanges regarding methodology and adaptations to Brazilian context
- Three day workshop hosted by CPRN for the Brazil dialogue team, Ottawa. Topics covered: deliberative dialogue design methods, issues framing, preparation, analysis and reporting.
- Ongoing exchange via e-mail and teleconference to tailor a deliberative dialogue process and questions for the Brazilian context.

October – December 2004:
Dialogue Design – Workbook and Methodology
- Three day youth dialogue planning workshop in Rio de Janeiro hosted by Brazilian team, with participation by CPRN and IDRC (December). Workshop included regional teams involved with the implementation of the regional dialogues. Focus: development of the workbook and dialogue design – adaptation of methodology to Brazilian context and expertise.

January – May 2005:
Dialogue Planning, Preparation and Implementation
- Workshops in Rio de Janeiro with CPRN providing support and advice to the Brazil Project team leaders and regional teams to further refine the workbook and the dialogue methodology, prepare the facilitation and analysis teams as well as fine tune the implementation plan.
- CPRN advice during implementation phase, with increased activity as the analysis intensified (e.g., assistance with data collection tools, facilitation guides and templates, participant recruitment).
- Learnings from the Brazil project (youth appropriate dialogue design and materials) helped inform CPRN's youth dialogue planning.

June – August 2005:
Analysis and Reporting
- Joint CPRN- Brazilian research team meetings in Rio de Janeiro to review findings and the draft report, assess lessons learned, successes and challenges of the dialogue project.
- Verbal and written input through e-mail exchange.
- Refinements to Canadian youth dialogue design and materials drawing on Brazil experience.

September – December 2005:
IDRC extends contract with CPRN to achieve two additional purposes
1. Translation of the final report into English to facilitate a more comprehensive review of the process and results.
2. Organize a Brazil-Canada seminar to share methodological and substantive findings emerging from the Brazil project and CPRN's' National Youth Dialogue and Summit.
   - Final report *Juventude Brasileira e Democracia: participação, esferas e políticas públicas* released December 2005.

January 2006:
World Social Forum events in Caracas, Venezuela
- CPRN accepted the invitation of Ibase and POLIS to give joint presentations at two WSF events: a seminar on *Youth and democracy: participation, spheres and public policies* and a *Workshop on Dialogues for democratic consolidation*. CPRN's presentations focus on the results of the National Dialogue and Summit while the Brazil project team shared its research findings from the Brazil youth dialogue.

March 2006:
Joint Brazil Canada Seminar in Ottawa
- Brazil-Canada Seminar: *Strengthened Democracies and Engaged Youth in Brazil and Canada – Youth Dialogues, Methodologies, Results, and Policy Implications* held in Ottawa, March 27, 2006. Brazil participants: Dialogue Project Team [Pólis and Ibase], a youth dialogue participant from Rio de Janeiro, a representative of the Brazilian government, National Youth Secretariat. Canadian participants: a youth dialogue participant from the Dialogue and Summit, CPRN's dialogue project team, academics, government officials and IDRC officials.

January – April 2007:
The collaboration continues with this book and ongoing discussions

Supporting successful collaboration and shared learning: key factors

In our view the following factors contributed significantly to successful collaboration.

Shared belief in and commitment to the role of youth in strengthening democracy

The research organizations engaged with this project were motivated by a common interest: a desire to strengthen democratic practice and institutions in their respective countries through more effective engagement of young people in civil society and political life. Research in both countries revealed a worrisome trend of declining youth participation and lack of interest in formal political activities. We also shared the view that current research left significant gaps in our understanding of why young people's participation was declining, what would motivate them to become more politically engaged, and the policy levers required to address the problems. The dialogue projects in Brazil and Canada sought to fill some of these gaps by directly engaging with young people on these issues. While the socioeconomic and political contexts for Brazilian and Canadian youth differ in many respects, our common belief in the value of connecting with young people in a respectful and meaningful way to explore their realities and their aspirations created common ground within which to work together. This shared context and motivation enriched the collaboration.

Respecting and building on Brazilian experience and expertise

As Canadian collaborators, we were well aware of the many and significant Brazilian contributions and innovations to the field of community dialogue and civic engagement. These includes the internationally renowned work of Paulo Freire, pioneering participatory budgeting initiatives in Porto Alegre and other municipalities, and the rich history of solidarity and public mobilization campaigns, most notably around HIV-AIDS.[6] Moreover, the two Brazilian partners – Ibase and Pólis - are well recognized advocacy and research organizations with excellent track records in Brazil and abroad. This collective experience and expertise conditioned the way in which we approached our role as partners.

We worked to expand our knowledge of the Brazilian context, and to more fully understand the objectives, parameters, challenges and opportunities characterizing the Brazilian youth dialogue. Through an iterative and interactive approach, we collaborated on methods, materials, planning, analysis and reporting. In contrast to a 'knowledge or technology transfer' approach, we adopted what may be described as a 'co-creation' strategy: we worked together at developing a tailored dialogue design and materials appropriate for the particularities and needs of Brazilian reality, and in doing so learned from one another. The reciprocal nature of the collaboration – featuring mutual learning opportunities for Canada and Brazil – meant that this was much more than a routine contractual relationship involving a simple transfer of expertise and information from the contracted party to the contractor.

Bringing together theory and practice: policy, researchers and practitioners

The team assembled by Ibase and Pólis to plan, implement and report on the youth dialogue project included a network of regional teams including researchers from different disciplines (education, sociology, journalism, political studies), practitioners, youth/community service providers and youth advocates. While all shared commitment to the project, the actors brought quite distinct and different perspectives and motivations to the partnership. For some, influencing government policies and programs was a key driver, while others were more interested in probing new theoretical research questions and methodologies or using the results to support local actions.

This combination of actors in Brazil made for a lively if sometimes challenging milieu in which diverse and interdisciplinary perspectives were in creative tension with one another. The project team was able to manage this tension effectively by engaging and synthesizing these various perspectives. As a result, there was rigorous attention given to both process/design outcomes and to substantive policy outcomes.[7] The spirit of inquiry and intellectual curiosity that the researcher/practitioner/community workers networks demonstrated led to constructive challenging of process design and policy outcomes. It also made for a much richer collaboration than would have otherwise resulted.

Building relationships and trust

Face to face meetings and workshops involving key members of the Brazil project team, IDRC's Federico Burone and CPRN – both in Canada and in Brazil, from the onset and throughout the project - allowed team members to develop the relationships and trust necessary for successful collaboration. Working visits to each others' countries allowed us to get to know each other in our respective cultural and social contexts. This greatly assisted CPRN in tailoring advice and assistance to best meet the needs of the Brazilian team. A high degree of trust developed over time as the team got to know each other both professionally and on a personal level - from visiting a favela and dancing the samba together in the streets of Rio, making maple candy in the snow in rural Quebec, navigating the narrow streets of old Montreal, and of course sampling each others' culinary specialties. This facilitated communication despite the challenges posed by language.

Dialogue challenges in Brazil and how they were addressed

From the onset, the Brazilian project team was curious and keen to learn about dialogue methodologies used by CPRN, particularly that employed in the *Citizens' Dialogue on the Future of Canada: A 21st Century Social Contract*. They were also very much concerned with ensuring that the methodology would be relevant to their cultural and political context. They expressed a number of 'doubts' and concerns linked to how to adapt the methodology to Brazil's particular challenges and were forthright in sharing them with us.

These included:

- Brazil is very diverse, large and populous: its geography, cultures, racial make up, class and socio-economic differences, colonial past and political history presented challenges in designing a national dialogue: The challenge revolved around planning and executing a national research initiative that balanced the competing imperatives of a common approach and methodology with the need to tailor for regional realities and contexts. We collectively and individually wondered about how to design the dialogue to be adaptable to such a regionally diverse context. To give some idea of the different scales: CPRN's dialogues in Canada typically involved day-long dialogue sessions in 10-12 cities across the country engaging about 40 participants in each, for a total between 400-500. The Brazilian Youth dialogue project involved 40 dialogue sessions (five in each of eight provinces) engaging over 1000 youth.

- Recruiting a representative sample of the youth population: a logistical and methodological challenge: The project team needed to reach youth in favelas where many families do not have telephones and cannot be contacted by recruitment methods normally used in Canada. Beyond the sampling and logistical considerations (CPRN uses a professional polling firm for random recruitment, whereas in Brazil they used their networks), the more important challenge related to the gulf between rich and poor youth in Brazil. Dialogue methodology requires a coming together of socially and economically diverse group of youth to engage and deliberate together – and yet in Brazil interaction across classes is not frequent. We collectively struggled with questions about how to ensure that youth would be able to express themselves and engage in respectful dialogue across the very wide social divide between rich and poor.

- Literacy challenge: A dialogue workbook, containing factual information and values-based approaches or choices to foster deliberation, is a key element of the deliberative dialogue methodology used by CPRN. It assumes that most dialogue participants are able to read and are comfortable working with printed text as one of the principal sources of information. The literacy rate of youth in Brazil is considerably lower than in Canada. This raised a host of issues about how to adapt the workbook as a tool in the Brazilian context, so as to appeal to youth across the class and cultural divides.

- Adapting facilitation approaches in small groups and plenary sessions: CPRN's dialogues typically rely on self-facilitation by participants in small groups, with participants reporting back to plenary, and on professional facilitation in plenary sessions. Would this approach work with Brazilian youth or might they require facilitation in small groups as well? The team wrestled with how to facilitate a respectful and productive dialogue with 40 youth on choices they want to make and trade-offs they are prepared to accept.

- Moving from process to outcomes to actions: An ongoing challenge faced by both the Brazilians and Canadians is how to design and execute a dialogue so as to build and maintain momentum to effect change beyond the dialogue events, into community and policy actions. This issue was a preoccupation for the team throughout our collaboration on the design, execution, analysis and reporting on the results.

In addition to the challenges posed by methodology, tight timelines (less than 12 months to undertake and report on the dialogue), and the ambitious scope of the project, the language challenges facing the team were not negligible with a mix of Portuguese, English and French used throughout the project.

The authors and CPRN were very impressed with the Brazilian project team's ability to learn while doing, accommodating a second language (English), adapting the methodology to their realities while ensuring the integrity of the approach. IDRC played an important role in supporting this success - building on its international experience, it provided for face to face exchanges, with interpretation when necessary and for translation of documents.

Methodological adaptations 'made in Brazil'

- Decentralized approach:
  While CPRN's practice had been to use a small core team of facilitators and researchers to plan and execute its dialogues, the Brazil project team opted for a decen-

tralized approach. The national team identified and built a network of eight regional teams to plan the dialogues, recruit the youth participants, organize and facilitate 40 dialogues sessions (five each in the eight provinces), and analyze the findings for their region/province. Each regional team included community activists with experience in animation of community groups and academics/researchers, most with some background and interest in youth related issues and some with experience in facilitating youth focus groups.

- Shared responsibility - core national team and regional networks:
  The core Ibase/Pólis team brought the regional networks together in workshops (with CPRN and IDRC participation) to develop and create commitment to the dialogue methodology and analysis plan - including workbook content, dialogue process facilitation, data collection and analysis - so as to achieve comparable methods in each region. Each regional team provided the core project team with an analysis of their respective dialogue results and participated in subsequent discussions and workshops to review and interpret the overall dialogue results. Several members of the core project team (including external academics and Ibase/Pólis staff) analyzed and synthesized regional results to produce a draft report.

- Tapping Brazil's cultural expression to enrich the dialogue:
  The project team built on Brazil's deep tradition of cultural expression to enrich its dialogue materials and approach. This included a video to complement the workbook, an accessible and lively workbook, youth participants' use of story telling, poetry and song to express

their views during the dialogue and the production of engaging print and broadcast materials to promote the dialogue results to a mass audience.

- Strategic communications and outreach of results: Using the journalistic expertise of Ibase, the project team succeeded in widespread coverage of the dialogue results in regional daily newspapers across Brazil and in the broadcast media (both radio and television). Using youth participants to tell the story in major metropolitan centres across Brazil, they achieved a broad reach.

How this collaboration influenced CPRN's dialogue with youth

Engaging youth in issue identification and dialogue planning

Our Brazilian colleagues' concern about framing issues for their dialogue in terms that connect to young people's realities and with suitable language further stimulated CPRN to find new ways to identify and frame the issues to be explored in its own youth dialogue: *National Dialogue and Summit: Engaging Young Canadians in What Matters to Them.* To that end, CPRN convened an advisory group of leaders from national and local youth organizations to help frame the issues. These leaders, many in their 20s and early 30s, urged CPRN to directly engage youth up front and throughout the entire dialogue process. Heeding this advice, CPRN partnered with several youth-based organizations to launch an online survey to test issues identified by the Advisory Committee.

This was followed by a workshop to engage with a diverse group of youth from across Canada to further test and explore the identified issues (learning, work, environment and health) from their perspectives. They also provided advice about youth learning needs, including language and presentation and the kinds of facilitated processes that would engage them most in dialogue. Several youth workshop participants continued their involvement, reviewing the content of the workbook to ensure clarity of content, language level and lexicon. Additionally several young Advisory Committee members joined the Youth Dialogue and Summit facilitation team.

The advice from this workshop was reinforced by examples from our Brazilian colleagues. Their dynamic video and illustrated workbook inspired us to develop two illustrated workbooks (Section 1 – Background - Snapshot of Canada; Strengths and Challenges; How Canadians Govern Themselves and Section 2 – Dialogue Issues: Leaning, Work, Health and Environment)[8] that were a significant departure from our previous workbooks. Learning from Brazil's use of artistic/cultural expression, CPRN introduced a variety of media and arts in the process, including facilitated collective drumming as a metaphor for dialogue, graphic recording, and creative reporting back, such as theatre and rap (which young participants themselves initiated).

Youth in leadership roles

Discussions with our Brazilian colleagues about the facilitation of small groups and plenary deliberations coupled with similar input from CPRN's Advisory Committee led us to adapt its usual dialogue process (e.g., providing facilitators for small group deliberations and adopting peer to peer facilitation, with professional coach facilitators). Given that one of the overarching objectives of the dialogue was to empower young people to participate in democratic processes, it was decided to involve them throughout the dialogue process, including facilitating small group discussions and co-facilitating large group dialogues and plenary sessions. Following the example set by the Brazilian team, a pre-dialogue facilitators' workshop was held, where the youth facilitators worked through a draft design, and were assigned to four teams (three young people and one coach in each team). These teams worked together prior to and throughout the dialogue.

Two youth facilitators – one French speaker and one English speaker – served as emcees throughout the three and a half day dialogue, welcoming the 144 youth participants who came from all corners of Canada. A team of youth facilitators presented the background on the dialogue issues - work, education, environment, health and youth engagement – illustrated with colorful and imaginative visuals. CPRN reviewed their presentations to ensure accuracy of content, but their language and visuals were entirely their own.

Beyond the research report: building commitment to action

The desire by both CPRN and our Advisory Committee to effect change beyond the dialogue events – to be a catalyst for action by youth, institutions and policy makers - led to innovation. Decision makers from public, private and civil society organizations joined the young participants in the third day of the dialogue first to learn from the participants about the kind of Canada they want, to explore together recommendations for moving forward on the substantive issues, and to sharpen thinking on roles and responsibilities for various actors in society (governments, businesses, not-for-profit and community groups), as well as young people themselves. Participation by decision makers in a respectful dialogue with youth (following their own intense two day deliberations) modeled a different kind of relationship that is possible between youth and decision makers in a democracy.

At the end of the event, youth and decision makers alike were invited to make a commitment to action beyond the event. They captured their commitments in a letter to themselves with one copy posted on a Commitment Wall and the other mailed to them out about six weeks after the dialogue event. The dialogue results were captured in two reports – one in the voice of the young people, that presents their vision and values, and the actions they feel are needed to achieve their vision. The other is a more traditional research report, which includes quantitative and qualitative analysis of the results by CPRN, and provides policy implications and recommendations. The reports have been widely disseminated and are publicly available on CPRN's website, where they have been downloaded over 30,000 times. Unfortunately, CPRN was not nearly as successful as Brazil in attracting media coverage of either the dialogue itself or the results. This is an area for further learning from Brazil.

Since the reports were released (in early 2006), CPRN has launched a research series to expand knowledge about youth civic and political participation with the goal of identifying policy and community actions to encourage and support greater participation.[9]

Successes and reflections

Process and policy outcomes

The Brazil youth dialogue project succeeded in effectively adapting CPRN's deliberative dialogue method to its own context and in producing results that can help decision makers and civil society groups better integrate Brazilian youth in their society and democracy. The extent to which policymakers act upon the policy recommendations and directions identified in the dialogue report *(Brazilian Youth and Democracy: Participation, Spheres and Public Policies)* remains to be seen. However, responses to date are encouraging. Follow up initiatives are underway with a focus on educational reforms as a key step in enabling fuller civic participation. In addition Ibase and Pólis are launching a new Latin American youth and democracy project that builds on what they learned from the Brazilian dialogue. It will be important to be able to identify what concrete impact the dialogue results have on policies over time to integrate youth into Brazilian society and to report publicly on them.

New networks leverage action

The creation of new national and regional networks of social action, policy research and community-based organizations with a shared interest in and capacity for public engagement and dialogue work is an important and unexpected outcome of the project, with potential for further collaboration and learning. This network building is an innovation that has good potential for replication in other Latin American countries. It demonstrates the benefits of combining on-the-ground community service with academic research to enrich both fields of endeavour. This fruitful nexus produced more than would have resulted from a traditional research approach. Moreover, the bridges created with decision makers in government offer potential for influencing policy formation and delivery of programs at different levels of government, in order to effect concrete change, for the benefit of young people and all of society.

Reflections on moving forward

Strengthening democratic practice, particularly by engaging youth, is a societal imperative everywhere. If we agree with this premise, then civil society organizations, researchers, activists, politicians and funders share a responsibility to critically examine our work to make sure it is really helping to deepen and improve democratic practices that in turn will make for stronger democracies.

Building on the Brazil-Canada collaborative partnership and our collective experiences with deliberative dialogues, what areas require particular attention if we are to improve our work and demonstrate it is making a difference? We offer the following five areas of dialogue theory and practice for consideration.

1. Focus on the quality of deliberative processes: we need to create meaningful, relevant processes that engage young people on issues of greatest concern to their everyday lives. This includes offering learning opportunities, preparing them to consider and make informed choices, and supporting their responsible actions as citizens in addressing those challenges. We need to find better ways to reach and engage youth, on issues they care about, in language they understand, with a variety of media and means of cultural expression. Critical reflection on our work, further experimentation building on lessons learned and continued exchange will no doubt contribute to improving the quality of deliberative processes.

2. Ensure that youth have a role in framing the issues for dialogue, in the design and facilitation of dialogues, and dissemination of results in their own environments: if we insist on controlling the content, agenda, process and reporting, then we will fail because we will reproduce the kind of adult/expert centric world in which they feel marginalized rather than empowered. To create the change needed in democratic practice in our countries, we need to model the kind of relationship that supports good democratic practice, including a different way of relating across generations: between young people and 'older' decision/policy makers, youth and adult facilitators, youth as social actors and 'adult' researchers. Our experience to date has shown that engaging youth at all stages of the process – from issues framing to report-

ing – makes for more relevant policy research and it benefits youth as well since they learn, develop confidence in themselves, and strengthen their resolve to participate as citizens. This is not an either/or choice. We need to do better at identifying and implementing ways of achieving both purposes well.

3. Work to improve the quality of policy research: critically examining and improving the rigor of process, data collection instruments, analytic methods and replicability will help build credibility with policymakers, and community actors. This takes resources, intellectual work and time. To contribute to research we need to encourage greater sharing of methods and tools through new venues that promote conversation and innovation. This will help us innovate and improve practice within our own countries and in collaboration with others abroad.

4. Give greater attention to evaluation: while the field has not yet arrived at broadly accepted frameworks for evaluation (though considerable progress is being made),[10] it is nonetheless important to build in flexible measures to assess the quality of the deliberation, of the analysis and the impact of dialogue results. Wherever possible, conducting follow up assessments with the dialogue participants and with policymakers to examine the influences and effects on individual engagement in public participation beyond the dialogues, as well as the contribution of the dialogue reports and outreach on policy/program formulation at different levels (national, state/provincial, and local) is highly desirable. More systematic approaches to evaluation of impacts on policy and on participants would do much to build credibility in academic, policy and community arenas. We need to build a body of evidence to support the growth and professionalization of the field.

5. Most importantly, work to build and maintain momentum beyond dialogue events to effect change: young people are sceptical of initiatives that fail to connect to action and some policymakers are dubious about experiential evidence and are dismissive of one-off initiatives. We need to be both thoughtful and creative in synthesizing dialogue results in a way that promotes action by all actors in society. We also need to improve our methods of dissemination to maximize opportunities to leverage results for concrete actions.

Every day the media bombard us with local, nation and international stories portraying disengagement, conflict, and violence, amplifying differences across communities and generations. Mainstream media rarely discusses dialogue and deliberation as an effective way to go about solving societal problems. Fortunately, there are encouraging signs of growing interest in the practice of dialogue and deliberation among politicians, researchers and the public in a number of countries. Groundbreaking initiatives are underway in Europe, Asia, Australia and the Americas, in addition to those discussed in this paper that demonstrate the value of these methods in addressing the wicked problems facing society, strengthening communities and the practice of democracy.

However, there is no guarantee that public engagement and the practice of dialogue and deliberation will necessarily take off. If we are going to make it more than an interesting novelty, sustained efforts are needed to shift the way we engage with each other at home and globally around collective problem solving. This will take commitment by practitioners, researchers and funders. The experience of this Canada-Brazil project gives us renewed energy to pursue this goal with passion and determination.

In closing, we applaud IDRC for taking the initiative to sponsor and publish the experience and results of the Brazilian youth dialogue. The Centre is setting an example of capturing and sharing knowledge as a foundation for continued efforts in exploring how to foster and improve deliberative dialogue.

We also salute our Brazilian colleagues for their vision and commitment and for welcoming us to join their learning journey on what we believe is a pathway to strengthened democracy.

Chapter 7

NETWORKED RESEARCH
A Decentralized, Participatory Study

*Sebastião Soares**

The Choice Work Dialogue methodology is underpinned by values and concepts that, in their essence, offer a certain kind of setup for conducting research. It enables a diversity of organizations and institutions with different outlooks to take part in forming a rich mosaic of analyses and thinking – what we will call here *networked research*.

These values and concepts can be grouped into three major, ethico-political and methodological sets. The first set reflects respect for, and valorization of diversities, both socio-cultural (ethnicities, beliefs and values, customs and choices) and regional (natural and acquired attributes and available resources, history, and state of economic, social and political development). The second has to do with democracy, pluralism and social participation in building states and systems of government. It is especially important for establishing social oversight of policy-making and monitoring policy implementation.

---

* Sebastião Soares is the technical coordinator of the study *Brazilian Youth and Democracy: Participation, Spheres and Public Policies* and chairman of Ibase's Advisory Board.

The third set relates to a methodological issue since public opinion can only form on any issue or subject if information is available and there are spaces and opportunities open where people can interact. This is a collective process of exchanging and sharing ideas. It is a process that involves bringing people's individual thinking in contrast and interaction with the thinking of others. The thinking involved relates to the participants' deepest-seated values, is influenced by their emotional reactions, and will finally be formulated by incorporating aspects, portions or slants of the views of various participants in the dialogue.

This methodology helps dialogue participants see themselves as subjects of their own history. It is therefore a research method which brings out and records opinions and perceptions which, at the same time, open up opportunities to shape these people.

In view of these values and concepts and given the characteristics of the study *Brazilian Youth and Democracy* (described in the Introduction to this book), especially its spread and complexity (the relatively short timeframe and parsimonious budget), the project was decentralized.

This decision was taken after intense discussion and thought by the technical and coordination teams from Ibase and Pólis, with the participation of the Canadian partners (IDRC and CPRN). Basically, decentralization entailed drawing on local organizations and professionals in each of the seven metropolitan regions and the Federal District where the study was carried out and setting up the specific teams that would be responsible for carrying out the study and analyzing the results in the respective region with them.

Right away two major risks were identified in this decision. Firstly, it might produce a 'patchwork' of results instead of a study with national scope as intended. Decentralization could lead to the dialogue methodology being applied differently or with uneven emphasis in the various regions. That would mean the results could neither be compared nor aggregated to yield the desired overview of the study population. Secondly, the decentralized research process might progressively lose cohesion - with methods and emphases not being uniformly applied; disparate progress rates leading to irretrievable delays in certain regions; and irregular quality levels in the work done and the results obtained. All of these could disqualify the study as a whole.

Nonetheless, there are numerous, important, albeit latent advantages to this approach. Among the benefits are that the study can be conducted by local groups of professionals who are familiar with regional characteristics and have greater confidence and credibility among the target public regarding the aims of the research. Young participants can realize more quickly and clearly what is being proposed to them, and perceive the legitimacy and ethical integrity of the process and those conducting it.

This approach also makes it possible to comprehensively and naturally grasp the exuberant diversity of the population, both socio-cultural and regional. As mentioned above, it matches fundamental values and concepts of the methodology. As shown by the results obtained in all the studied regions, this gain is very important both in terms of diagnosing deficits and problems, aspirations and opportunities, and also in terms of the conclusions and proposals yielded by the study.

The creation of a network of organizations and institutions attuned to the fundamental values and concepts of the methodology located at the study sites and decentralizing how the methodology was conducted had two major advantages. Firstly, it strengthened the regional organizations. Secondly, it developed institutional leadership capacity in the region which will be useful for future activities on this subject or others.

Providing care is taken to surmount and minimize the risks, decentralization certainly facilitates the work. Setting up a team of professionals located at either of the coordinating organizations (Ibase or Pólis) in Rio de Janeiro or São Paulo, which would then have to do the research on an itinerant basis in the various regions, would have resulted in larger budgets and longer timeframes. Brazil is a country of continental proportions, so travel to the regions and the need for the team to familiarize itself with regional situations would certainly have led to the study costing more and taking longer.

Two general observations must be made. Ibase and Pólis have systematically carried out joint work and work in coordination with other leading organizations and individuals on various issues. Ibase has worked in this way since the early days in the 1980s and 90s, during the Agrarian Reform Campaign and Citizens' Action (*Ação da Cidadania*). More recently, Ibase's and Pólis' activities have centred around networked setups, both in specific policy-implementation studies and other related work. They have also taken this approach when mobilizing and animating social actors to build a more just and egalitarian society (through the World Social Forum, for instance).

Meanwhile using the Choice Work Dialogue methodology IDRC and CPRN have carried out numerous studies in Canada on a wide variety of subjects. In each of these CPRN set up a team of professionals located in Ottawa, which then traveled to the various regions in order to conduct the study. Despite the differences in approaches, the Canadians understood perfectly well the reasons for decentralizing the work in Brazil by organizing a network of partners. They supported, and contributed decisively to, the minor modifications needed in order to apply this methodology under our circumstances. They also attentively accompanied the progress at all stages of the study and in the end, were wholly approving of the results obtained thereby confirming the correctness and merit of the adopted solution.

The logic of the network's structure and functioning

With a view to promoting North-South relations, building links in solidarity between our peoples, and investing in dialogue, respect for diversity and mutual listening, the first important partnership was struck between the Canadian (IDRC and CPRN) and Brazilian (Ibase and Pólis) organizations.

In Brazil, the basic, preliminary criterion for setting up the network was to find and interlink non-governmental organizations and institutions or groups engaged in academic extension activities. Two further criteria were also observed. The institutions, NGOs and university extension schemes, should be formally established and meet certain minimum requirements regarding knowledge of the issue from previous activities. They should also be recognized as ethically and professionally sound.

It was also desirable that the researchers have prior connection with the partner institutions and they were asked to submit curricula indicating the nature and results of that connection and its affinity with the purposes of the study.

In light of these criteria, the project sought to contact and connect with possible partners. Potential partners were identified through the Brazilian Association of Non-governmental Organizations (Abong) database, and from prior knowledge of Ibase and Pólis leaders, researchers and collaborators.

After reaching the necessary understandings and concluding negotiations between Ibase's leaders and the local organization, the partnership was formally constituted by contract. The project team members from each region were selected by résumé and, in some cases, through further telephone interviews. The criterion that team members should already be connected with the partner organization was maintained in all but a few cases. Our experience in this study reinforces the appropriateness of this rule, particularly for securing developments from the study in the local region.

Initially, with a view to lower costs and shorter timeframes, the two stages of the study would be carried out differently. The first, quantitative stage (an opinion poll of a sample of 8,000 young people in the seven regions and the Federal District), would be done by a statistics consultancy specialized in conducting nationwide public-opinion polls in Brazil, hired specifically for this purpose. The qualitative stage (40 Dialogue Group meetings in the same regions) would be carried out by teams of professionals set up especially for the purpose and managed by Ibase and Pólis.

As the final project matured and consolidated and the relationship with our Canadian partners did the same, preference shifted to a decentralized arrangement involving the network of partners for the quantitative stage of the study as well. A minor adjustment was also made to the approach of the quantitative study (outsourcing to a specialized firm). A decision was made to also involve the regional teams in the partner network in this stage. They would participate in discussions around and the preparation of the questionnaire used in the interviews of the 8,000 young people. They would also subsequently analyze the data collected, processed and tabulated by the outsourced firm, and draft the actual report on their respective region. This small adjustment proved fundamental to preventing any disconnect between the two stages of the study and to assuring the success of the project as a whole.

A regional team comprised of a supervisor and two research assistants was set up in each region. The supervisors and assistants began their work during the third and seventh month of project execution respectively. They remained active until the 18th month, when research activities practically came to an end and the results were presented at two scheduled events at the World Social Forum in Caracas, Venezuela in January 2006.

During the time when the Dialogue Group meetings were being held – approximately three months during the first half of 2005 – each regional team was reinforced by four intern researchers who participated in moderating the meetings and recording what happened during the various phases of the meetings. In all, 61 professionals took part in the eight regional teams including eight supervisors, 18 research assistants and 35 intern researchers.

Indispensable periodic workshops

The proper management of the sizeable body of researchers working in a decentralized study presented a major challenge. This challenge was successfully met with the aid of certain provisions on the organization and operation of the partner network. Workshops were a prominent component among these provisions. They brought the technical and coordination teams, supervisors and research assistants together in Rio de Janeiro for three days of activities. During the course of the 18 and a half months of the project, four workshops were held. Their timing and aims are described below.

The first took place early in the third month of the project's execution. Its purpose was to discuss the scope of the study (goals, stages, timeframes and products) in minute detail; to prepare and approve the detailed work schedule (activities, organization and procedures, participants' responsibilities, bi-weekly timetable, expected results); to start discussing the Dialogue Group (Choice Work Dialogue) methodology; and to discuss and finish preparing the 46-item questionnaire for the opinion poll for the quantitative stage of the study.

The second workshop, at the start of the sixth month of the project's execution, explored knowledge on the Dialogue Group methodology in greater depth, started the preparation of the tools for the qualitative stage (Facilitator's Guide, Dialogue Manual), evaluated progress in the early stage of the project and made some minor adjustments to the schedule, especially with a view to incorporating the research assistants into the regional teams.

The third workshop was held during the eighth month of the project's execution and was particularly important, because it included the participation of both the recently-engaged research assistants and an experienced Canadian consultant from CPRN. The emphasis of this workshop was on methodological issues, including conclusive discussions on the final versions of the tools for the Dialogue Groups. In addition, the preliminary schedule for these groups was set out, and criteria for group formation and participant selection were discussed, as well as procedures for contacting the young people and inviting them to take part. Lastly, the meeting discussed the processed, tabulated results of the opinion poll and the guidelines for reporting on this quantitative stage.

The fourth workshop took place during the 15th month of the project's execution. It discussed the final versions of the regional reports and the overall study report, with particular focus on the final topics, conclusions and recommendations. It also discussed the strategic plan for providing feedback on the results and publicizing them in the national and regional media. At this workshop, participants also debated extending and continuing the study and adjusting the programme in the final stages, as well as how to broaden the international dissemination of the results at the World Social Forum in Caracas.

The workshops were fundamental for the members of the teams to get to know each other and mesh, and for everyone involved to fully and homogeneously understand the scope of the study and its specific characteristics. They also contributed decisively to reducing the friction that naturally ensues in implementing any endeavour, but especially complex, large-scale ones.

Another essential measure was to ensure that the Dialogue Group methodology was fully absorbed, first by the technical team and then by the regional teams. In the latter case, exhaustive efforts were made to ensure that the regional teams reached a homogeneous understanding of all facets of the methodology. This was done so that the results obtained from this decentralized study would be consistent, as they in fact they were.

Transfer of the methodology first began in Canada when, with the support of CPRN and IDRC, four members of the technical team travelled north at the start of the project make a complete, concentrated study of all of its aspects. The methodology was then transferred to the regional teams - mainly at the workshops - with indispensable technical support from the Canadians.

Collective construction

The method followed from the outset was for the work tools to be constructed collectively by all the professionals involved. Final drafting of the opinion-poll questionnaire and the guidelines for the various reports, as well as preparation of the Facilitator's Guide, the Dialogue Manual, the Pre- and Post-Dialogue Forms, the banners and the CD-ROM (developed for the Dialogue Groups) were all jointly developed, discussed, adjusted until reaching their final form. This form may not have corresponded to what many considered ideal, but it was of a quality sufficient for their intended purposes. Once accepted, they were immediately appropriated and used by all who had collaborated in moulding them.

This collective construction method of the work tools greatly contributed to avoiding the risks inherent in conducting the study through a network of regional partners. The continuous planning and programming of the research activities, careful monitoring and periodic review of progress by all teams and, above all, the minimization of alterations to what had already been decided, especially the execution timeframes for the various stages, helped eliminate the risk of losing cohesion during the course of the study.

In fact, the arrangement adopted for the study was for the execution to be decentralized, but for the planning to be centralized although intensely participatory. These methods account largely for the project's success.

This planning and supervision effort was anchored in the technical and coordination teams, but was always performed with frequent, intense consultation and discussions with all the teams in the partner network. This was done through the periodic workshops, by telephone, and mostly through the e-forum and other specific announcements and messages over the Internet.

The e-forum was accessible and available to all project participants including the coordinating organizations, the network of partner organizations and all participating professionals. During the course of the study, the forum rendered outstanding services suited to each stage of project implementation. Thus, in the early days, it played a key role in communicating the project and its – especially methodological – characteristics; circulating and sharing the researchers' opinions; and generally 'breaking the ice' among those professionals engaged in the project.

At the time that the Dialogue Groups were being held, it served as an extensive and diversified framework for sharing the 'torrent' of experiences by the various teams. It created a common environment of outstanding solidarity which was frequented by everyone and it was used to draw energy from when facing common difficulties.

In the final stages of the study, it was indispensable in developing the reports, arranging the feedback of results to the young participants and local/regional publics, in implementing the strategic media plan, and in coordinating the teams' participation in the World Social Forum in Caracas.

All in all, the e-forum established an efficient pattern of real-time communication and constituted a paradigm of transparency among partners and professionals participating in the study on all the subjects and issues relating to it.

The procedures and routines set up at the outset of the project all ensured an effective system of quality control of the work done in each and every region where the study was carried out. These include the clearly assigned responsibilities of all the professionals involved in the study; the collectively-constructed work tools and reporting guidelines; the frequent orientations given by the technical team; the debates and discussions at the workshops and through the e-forum; the effort put into managing the technical teams and coordination; and, above all, the unquestionable and generalized competence and dedication of the regional teams.

The network

In order to help understand the composition of the network set up to perform the research, some general information on the organizations that constituted the network is presented below. This information also includes a summary of the main activities they engage in, as well as information about the professionals – coordinators, consultants, technical staffs, supervisors and research assistants – who made up the overall, national and regional teams.

Overall Project Coordination

Instituto Brasileiro de Análises Sociais e Econômicas (Ibase):
- Overall coordinator: Itamar Silva
- Technical coordinator: Sebastião Soares
- Technical team: Patrícia Lânes, Eliane Ribeiro, Paulo Carrano

- Statistics advisors: Marco Antônio Aguiar, Leonardo Méllo, Márcia Tibau
- Secretaries: Inês Carvalho and Rozi Billo

Ibase is a not-for-profit institution set up in 1981. Its mission is to build democracy by combating inequalities and stimulating citizens' participation. Its areas of activity include the World Social Forum process, democratic alternatives to globalization, monitoring public policy, democratizing the city, food security, solidarity economy, and social accountability and ethical responsibility in organizations.

Its target publics include social and grassroots movements; community organizations; active citizen leaders, groups and organizations; schools, students and teachers; community radios and alternative communication endeavours; opinion leaders in the mass media; members of parliaments and their advisors; and policy-makers.

Instituto de Estudos, Formação e Assessoria em Políticas Sociais (Pólis):
- Overall deputy coordinator: Anna Luiza Salles Souto

Pólis is a non-governmental organization which has been active at the Brazilian national level since its foundation in 1987. It is closely identified with urban issues and the field of public policy and local development. Citizens' rights as an achievement of democracy is the central theme by which it organizes its activities, which are directed to ensuring that cities are just, sustainable and democratic.

The Institute's activities include research, courses and advisory services, and it forms part of citizens' rights advocacy coalitions and networks. Their specific key areas are participatory citizenship, food and nutritional security, urbanism and the right to the city, public-policy monitoring, urban environment, culture and local economic development.

Technical and financial support

International Development Research Centre (IDRC):
- Coordinator: Federico Burone

The International Development Research Centre (IDRC) is a public corporation created by the Parliament of Canada in 1970 to help developing countries use science and technology to find practical, long-term solutions to the social, economic, and environmental problems they face.

Support is directed toward strengthening local capacity in developing countries with a view to furthering the research, policies and technologies needed to build more equitable societies.

In carrying out its mission, IDRC provides funds and expert advice to developing-country researchers working to solve critical development problems. The broad themes addressed are environment and natural resource management; information and communication technologies for development; innovation, policy and science; and social and economic policy.

IDRC organizes partnerships between nations of the South and various kinds of Canadian organizations – universities, trade unions, social movements and so on. IDRC also funds studies and research by academics from Canada and developing countries. Its offices are in Ottawa and it has six regional offices in Montevideo (Uruguay), Dakar (Senegal), Nairobi (Kenya), Cairo (Egypt), New Delhi (India) and Singapore.

Technical and methodological support

Canadian Policy Research Networks (CPRN):
- Coordinator: Mary Pat MacKinnon
- Consultant: Suzanne Taschereau

Canadian Policy Research Networks is a non-profit organization based in Ottawa. CPRN was founded in 1994 by Judith

Maxwell, former Chair of the Economic Council of Canada, at a time when the advance of neoliberalism and international economic crises raised concerns over maintaining social gains in Canada.

CPRN's mission is to create knowledge and lead public dialogue and debate on social and economic issues to strengthen social rights. CPRN conducts research to provide information and analytical input to policy-making, bringing together NGOs, universities, trade unions, business associations and government. It provides a neutral space where a variety of social stakeholders can dialogue and share their thinking on public policies.

Its priority areas are children and youth; citizen engagement; democracy, governance and citizenship; diversity; education and learning; health, labour market; job quality; and social protection.

CPRN's website offers free publications in its areas of activity. In 2006, there were approximately 1.9 million downloads of this material.

Partner in Porto Alegre, Rio Grande do Sul:
Universidade Federal do Rio Grande do Sul (UFRGS)

Porto Alegre regional team:
- Supervisor: Nilton Bueno Fischer
- Research assistants: Carmem Zeli Vargas Gil Souza, Nara Vieira Ramos, Nilda Stecanela and Sueli Salva

The Rio Grande do Sul Federal University (UFRGS) is based in Porto Alegre which is the state capital of Rio Grande do Sul. Set up by State Decree No. 5,758 on 28 November 1934 and federalized by Law No. 1,254 on 4 December 1950, it is a self-regulating institution with autonomy in managing its scientific, teaching, administrative and financial and patrimonial affairs.

The main purpose of the UFRGS, its faculty, students and technical and administrative staff is higher education and the production of philosophical, scientific, artistic and technological knowledge through teaching, research and extension.

In that context its postgraduate programme in Education, in addition to offering advanced Master's and doctoral seminars on the subject of youth, has a faculty that researches the subject from a variety of theoretical and methodological approaches. These include media and youth; youth and leadership; youth in situations of risk (boys and girls on the streets and in public shelters); and youth and policy.

Master's and doctoral students have also researched youth for their theses, ranging from their spatial situation (on the streets and in school), their use of the media and computers (also youth and free time), to a variety of activities under the overall denomination of corporality and youth (dances and performances; *capoeira*[1] among young people, etc.). Studies have also been carried out of municipal policies and the management of programmes and actions, both on the initiative of youth movements and in partnership with them.

These studies take in the Porto Alegre metropolitan region, but in some cases also consider the interior of the state (Serra Gaúcha and the coastal region). Institutional studies are also carried out in partnership with other Brazilian institutions, such as in the case of the study Youth, Schooling and Local Power (*Juventude, escolarização e poder local*) in partnership with *Ação Educativa* in São Paulo, with funding from Fapesp/CNPq.

Partners in Rio de Janeiro, RJ:
Iser Assessoria: religião, cidadania e democracia
Observatório Jovem do Rio de Janeiro

Rio de Janeiro regional team:
- Supervisor: Solange dos Santos Rodrigues
- Research assistants: Alexandre da Silva Aguiar and Marilena Cunha

Iser Assessoria

Iser Assessoria is a not-for-profit association set up in 1995. Its fundamental commitment is to building a society grounded in freedom, justice and solidarity in Brazil. Brazilian society bears the imprint of profound inequalities, especially in access to information and knowledge, making it difficult for poorer sectors to participate as subjects in the process of consolidating democracy.

To address that situation, Iser promotes the circulation of knowledge in response to demands for capacity-building from individuals connected with social movements, the ecumenical movement and academic institutions. It conducts courses, studies, seminars and debates, and produces publications that circulate widely in Brazil. The central thread connecting these activities is the relationship between religious phenomena and democracy building process, including gender relations and youth as cross-cutting themes.

In recent years, emphasis has been given to participatory democracy, encouraging public participation in policy-making and monitoring policy implementation.

Five years ago, Iser began working specifically on youth and social participation with a view to supporting citizenship-building processes for young Brazilians. It advises on events organized by youth groups and organizations working with young people; gives courses, round tables and debates; does research; prepares input for workshops; conducts specific literature reviews; circulates official information; and dialogues with militants in youth movements, students of these issues and Members of Parliament.

Observatório Jovem do Rio de Janeiro

This Youth Observatory began its activities in 2001, as an outreach project connected with the Faculty of Education at Fluminense Federal University (UFF). In 2003, it became part of the postgraduate programme in Education, as an inter-institutional, multidisciplinary study, research and outreach group. In addition to professors, undergraduates and graduates, it includes faculty from other universities (UERJ, UNIRIO, UFRRJ) and social organizations (Ibase, Iser/Assessoria, Instituto Imagem e Cidadania) among others.

Its main study and research concerns relate to how the 'youth condition' has changed over time, the life situations of contemporary youth and their social, cultural and political mobilizations. It also keeps a critical eye on youth-policy developments.

The Observatory produces material of its own in the form of interviews and articles, and also circulates official information from other sources. Its website is intended to be a channel for encouraging dialogue among researchers of youth issues, and between them and society. The site hosts studies and other work by the Observatory and other groups, complete texts on a range of subjects, recommended reading, critical commentary, reviews, interviews, articles and newsletters – all from a scientific journalism standpoint.

Partner in São Paulo, SP:
Ação Educativa

São Paulo regional team:
- Supervisor: Ana Paula de Oliveira Corti
- Research assistants: Elizabete Regina Baptista de Oliveira and Raquel de Souza Santos.

Ação Educativa was founded in 1994 with the mission of contributing to effective educational and youth rights, with a view to promoting social justice, participatory democracy and sustainable development in Brazil.

It combines a variety of work and action strategies such as: local action and educational experimentation; training and capacity-building for young people, educators and other social agents; setting up and participating in networks and forums at the local and national levels; promotional campaigns; researching and disseminating information and knowledge; promoting debates and exchange; producing educational materials; advising government; lobbying the Executive, Legislative and Judiciary branches of government, and related advocacy activities.

In relation to youth, Ação Educativa both helps youth groups and forums function and interrelate while also organizing training activities. In addition it supports the structuring and development of youth policies. In its activities with young people, it seeks to strengthen their capacity for collective action. In capacity-building activities, it begins with the interests expressed by young people in order to support them in preparing and implementing the projects.

Ação Educativa gives special attention to establishing dialogue with other civil society actors (community organizations and other NGOs) and with government either by building partnerships or by conveying demands. It does so both in its training activities for young people and when advising youth groups and fostering and supporting networks and forums of youth organizations. Since dialogue is not only difficult for young people, they apply the same idea when carrying out training activities or when providing the advisory services to governments, educators and NGOs.

Partners in Recife, Pernambuco:
Equip
Projeto Redes & Juventudes

Recife regional team:
- Supervisor: Lívia De Tommasi
- Research assistants: Graça Elenice dos Santos Braga and Marcílio Dantas Brandão

Equip

Founded in July 1988, the Escola de Formação Quilombo dos Palmares (Equip) grew out of the maturity and organization achieved by trade union and grassroots movements in northeast Brazil during the 1970s and 1980s. Its history intertwines with the histories of struggle and resistance by northeastern trade-union and grassroots leaders.

It is a non-governmental organization that invests in training activities and in interchanging and systematically recording grassroots education activities. It proposes the dissemination of grassroots education, placing emphasis to methodological capacity-building for grassroots movements and organizations.

Projeto Redes & Juventude

This group proposes setting up and organizing a network of 25 NGO-run projects with youth, most of which are based in northeastern Brazil. The focus of this network's activities is youth participation in advocacy. The project is hosted by Save the Children in Recife.

They organize debates and workshops on youth-related issues such as placement in the work market, the solidarity economy, action methodology, and communication. They take part in local and national events to discuss youth policies, such as the National Youth Conference (*Conferência Nacional de Juventude*), and meetings organized by Projeto Juventude, which is run by the Instituto de Cidadania.

Partner in Brasília, DF:
Inesc

Brasília regional team:
- Supervisor: Ozanira Ferreira da Costa

- Research assistants: Karina Aparecida Figueiredo and Perla Ribeiro

Set up in 1979, the mission of the Instituto de Estudos Socioeconômicos (Inesc) is 'to contribute to strengthening participatory democracy, with a view to ensuring human rights, by monitoring and evaluating public policies, mainly with regard to Brazil's national Congress'.

For these purposes, it pursues activities that range from drafting and monitoring proposed laws, monitoring budget preparation and execution, and coordinating with other civil-society organizations.

Inesc is active on the following main issues: children and adolescents; agrarian and agricultural policies; indigenous peoples and environment; public spending; and international politics.

Partner in Belo Horizonte, MG:
Observatório da Juventude, Universidade Federal de Minas Gerais (UFMG)

Belo Horizonte regional team:
- Supervisor: Juarez Tarcísio Dayrell
- Research assistants: Geraldo Magela Pereira and Nilma Lino Gomes

The Youth Observatory is a teaching, research and outreach programme of the Education Faculty at Minas Gerais Federal University supported by the Outreach Department. Since 2002 it has been researching, surveying and distributing information on the situation of youth in the Belo Horizonte metropolitan region. It has also organized capacity-building exercises both for young people and for educators and undergraduates at UFMG interested in youth issues.

The programme forms part of the affirmative-action policy context, and is guided by four key directions that delimit its institutional action: the 'youth condition'; policies and social actions; cultural practices and collective action by young people in the city; and construction of methodologies for working with young people. The Observatory has conducted youth-related university outreach and research projects.

Partner in Salvador, BA:
Centro de Referência Integral de Adolescentes (Cria)

Salvador regional team:
- Supervisor: Júlia Taís Campos Ribeiro
- Research assistants: Ana Paula Carvalho da Silva and Fernanda Glória França Colaço

The Centro de Referência Integral de Adolescentes (Cria) is an NGO founded in February 1994. Based in the Pelourinho district, the historical centre of Salvador, its aim is to contribute to improving educational, health and cultural policies.

It works in the field of arts and education focussing on theatre staged by adolescents and young people from various areas of the city, especially those youth from poor districts who are studying at public schools. Its training activities for young people include an Education for Citizenship programme focussing on education, health and culture.

The young people and educators at Cria participate in social monitoring structures, such as Salvador's municipal forum and council on children's rights (*Fórum e Conselho Municipal dos Direitos da Criança e Adolescente*), the National Youth Network (*Rede Nacional de Juventude*) and the Latin and Caribbean Youth Network (*Rede Latino-americana e Caribenha de Juventude*). It also interlinks with other NGOs to form and animate a state youth forum. In addition, it has actively participated at the government level with the Salvador Youth Coordination Department (*Coordenadoria da Juventude*).

Partner in Belém, Pará:
Unipop

Belém regional team:
- Supervisor: Lúcia Isabel da Conceição Silva
- Research assistants: Francisca Guiomar Cruz da Silva and Rosely Risuenho Viana

In 1987, a total of 15 institutions in Belém including organizations connected with the grassroots and trade-union movements and religious institutions, founded Unipop. Unipop is a grassroots education NGO whose guiding principle is political, gender, cultural and religious pluralism. It is also an experimental initiative in education for citizenship, building on the socio-political, ecumenical-theological and ludic-theatrical approaches. Their specific work with young people started in 1999 when it was defined as a priority public for its training activities.

Final remarks

Lastly, I would like to emphasize two important points. The work of this network ensured that the study *Brazilian Youth and Democracy: Participation, Spheres and Public Policies* achieved efficiency (the project kept within its timetable and budget), efficacy (all stages of the study were completed in all the regions, to a high and uniform standard of quality) and effectiveness (reliable results were obtained which really expressed the characteristics of the study population). It also allowed all the project goals to be accomplished in full. There can also be no doubt that, with due regard for diversities, the organizational arrangements and the managerial solutions adopted in this study can be applied in similar undertakings in the future.

It must also be stressed that certain factors significantly contributed to greater equity in how the research network was constructed. These were: the institutions, organizations and professionals involved all had a significant background in research and knowledge on the issues; information circulated constantly; all stages of the research process were discussed (from developing the tools, analyzing the outcomes, through to disseminating the results); the experience and outlook of the NGOs and youth networks was combined with input from universities; and the organizations, institutions and researchers were committed to producing inputs for new public policies, strategies and actions directed to Brazilian youth.

In short, the network can be an important tool for facilitating the production of knowledge, at the same time as it contributes to providing visibility to, and reinforcing, important issues in the struggle for a less unequal world.

Chapter 8

BRAZILIAN YOUTH AND DEMOCRACY
The Press Campaign

Rogério Pacheco Jordão*

The first step to publicizing the *Brazilian Youth and Democracy* study – which began in November 2005 and was conducted in three stages over a one-year period – was to understand the nature of the survey. The study's goal was concrete and clearly defined since the study was designed to produce results that would influence public policies.

Another key facet of the survey was that it was intended to detect the opportunities for participation available to young people, with an eye on the democratization process underway in Brazilian society. It was not simply designed to profile young people in the major urban centres, such as other work carried out and published on youth in recent times. From the onset these two features pointed to two key target audiences: public policy-makers from throughout Brazil and young people themselves.

Once these parameters had been laid out, the press advisors worked to give the greatest possible exposure to the

---

* Rogério Jordão is a journalist and press advisor to Ibase.

study's results and conclusions. They also worked to bring official information to the general public and, more importantly, to these interested groups. One constant concern voiced from the onset of the study was how to minimize the risk inherent in making any study public, which is the mistaken or distorted interpretation of the results. Therefore, the challenge became how to best make the results and conclusions 'newsworthy'.

Defining a strategy

A decision was made to avoid exclusivity (journalistic jargon for making the results available to only one publication or channel, with the idea of gaining more editorial coverage) with any media outlet. This decision guarded against the fear that if the interpretation was distorted a good part of the publicity work would also be undermined. Additionally, once material is published exclusively by one outlet, their competition is unlikely to be interested in the material and the results of the study are brought only to the attention of people who read one particular part of one particular newspaper.

The second step taken was to design a plan on how our regional partners would participate in publicizing the findings since the survey was conducted in seven metropolitan regions and the Federal District by various local organizations and institutions. The national press campaign was therefore designed to run in coordination with the local campaigns. The regional partners would work with their local data, but before they released this information to the local press, they would receive the interpreted national findings.

In some cases, the press office advised people by telephone on how to work effectively with the press, and what information to highlight and how to do so. The partners were e-mailed a step-by-step guide to getting press coverage. We all shared the single goal of ensuring the widest possible exposure without distorting the findings. Articles appeared in newspapers in all the metropolitan regions covered by the survey, adding to the wealth of interpretations.

The regional campaigns were an important step, which in addition to the national press, eventually secured a substantial presence in the press of all the metropolitan regions polled. With only rare exceptions, the regional campaigns followed the same lines as the national campaign, which was advantageous since it sent across a more clear-cut message.

Step-by-step

As soon as the report was finalized, the press advisors met with the national coordinators to draw out the study's key conclusions and information. Next, an eight-page press summary and draft a press release were prepared.

At first, the main key message communicated to the press was the phrase that opens the press release: 'Young people in the big cities are willing to participate more in public affairs and collective action – as long as these yield benefits to society (and suitable channels are available for them to participate).'

In the press summary we included the information about participation first. The survey showed a potential for participation, but it was only clear after a comparative reading of the final report. That is to say, although it was evident when the information was qualified, there was no single datum pointing to that conclusion. Therefore we highlighted the fact that, despite a clear disbelief in formal politics, the desire to participate was present although diffuse.

The information which we emphasized included data on opening up channels for dialogue (85 per cent agreed with the phrase 'Channels have to be opened up for dialogue between citizens and government'); following political affairs (65.6 per cent tried to keep themselves informed about politics); and how the Dialogue Groups were perceived – the qualitative stage of the study revealed that the young were eager to 'do something', especially actions with visible results.

Synthesizing the findings about participation was fundamentally important. Much of the data if taken in isolation could just confirm the common notion that young people are uninterested, which is certainly part of the truth. However, the real, original value of the study was just the opposite. It revealed a willingness to participate, and this provided an opening and opportunity for public policies.

There was no question of playing down what we did not want to show. In addition to the summary which was given to the press to facilitate the journalists' work, the full report was always available to anyone interested. Our intention was to organize the information so that it would be understood by a broader audience. The experience demonstrated how important it is to offer the press a self-explanatory and quickly understood summary of the results when working with this kind of study.

Results

Three press campaigns were run in the space of one year. The first was designed to win over political editorial staff. Generally speaking, the press faithfully reproduced the study's main findings. This was a bonus because it is not uncommon for journalists to pull out certain points and shift the interpretation.

The first newspaper to publish an article was *O Estado de São Paulo*, which has the fourth largest circulation in Brazil. Under the headline 'Youth disapprove of politicians', the reporter stressed that 'Most politicians do not represent the public's interests. That is the opinion of 64.7 per cent of young Brazilians. Nonetheless, 85 per cent of them feel that channels must be opened up for dialogue between citizens and government, because politics is an indispensable avenue for securing rights'.

That first news item – which very often has a cascade effect in influencing subsequent coverage – was helpful in that it emphasized the information on participation. Particularly it emphasized young people's understanding that dialogue is important, thereby countering the common notion that young are just not interested. In addition, it was strategically important that the article appeared in the newspaper's politics section, rather than the youth section, which is read by a more restricted public and whose coverage tends to be less political.

A few days later, a second piece came out, this time on the most-watched channel in the state and in Brazil, *RJTV* (the Rio de Janeiro news programme on TV Globo). It opened by saying that young people 'would like to participate more in public affairs'. The theme of participation was echoed by other leading media outlets. *Agência Brasil*, on the federal government's Radiobrás channel, titled the piece 'Survey signals young people's readiness to participate in politics'. *Folha Online*, the Internet portal of the daily *Folha de São Paulo*, posted an article headlined 'Young people show potential for participating in public affairs, says Ibase'.

Dozens of interviews were given to newspapers, TV channels and radio stations in Rio de Janeiro and São Paulo (the core sources of national coverage), as well as in the regions involved in the survey. This initial coverage had a crucial effect, because the press actually did interpret the findings in the same way as the researchers, helping to present the study in the correct light. One of the main challenges in putting a study across to the press is to manage to get the conclusions (and not just some random data taken in isolation) into the 'news'– and to get the media to help rather than hinder the process.

Ibase's review Democracia Viva

In February 2006, three months after the first articles were published, the survey reappeared in the press in the daily *Folha de São Paulo*, which has the largest circulation of any newspaper in Brazil. The interest of one of its journalists was rekindled after reading about the survey in Ibase's bimonthly review, *Democracia Viva*, which had devoted a special issue to the study. This example illustrates the importance of developing integrated communication strategies, where institutional communication – in this case, by Ibase – and press advisors work in harmony.

What prompted the article in the *Folha de São Paulo* was a graph published in *Democracia Viva* showing young people's occupation rates. This piece of information was highlighted, because it showed – and this was the paper's front-page headline – that '27 per cent of young people neither work nor study'. The prominence of the news piece spurred a new wave of exposure for the study – this time focusing not on participation, but on the realities facing young people in Brazil's big cities.

After the *Folha* article, the survey was mentioned a number of times over the next few months in opinion pieces and articles in a variety of newspapers and on radio programmes. Once again the regional partners played a key role as the local press began to contact them looking for a local angle on the numbers of young people who have no occupation.

TV and alternative media

The third wave of coverage came in August 2006, nearly one year after the survey's official launch. This time, it took place in the context of Brazil's presidential elections. The time was ripe because the researchers had now put together a primer of youth-policy proposals (the main aim of the whole exercise) based on the survey results. The booklet was circulated to policy makers all over Brazil and to the presidential candidates. This move helped kindle a new spark and generate news and bring the theme of youth into the electoral debate.

In this third stage, the information distributed centred on young people's demands and their proposals and it was captured by alternative press publications. The first to carry the news was *Brasil de Fato*, a left-wing newspaper with national circulation and penetration among social movements. This was followed by articles in *Agência Carta Maior* and in youth publications such as *Viração, Onda Jovem* and others.

Agência de Notícias do Direito da Infância (Andi, a children's rights news agency) made a significant contribution by redistributing Ibase's press release to its own mailing list. Andi, which commands enormous credibility among journalists and policy makers specializing in children and adolescents, even went so far as to use the research summary at a national seminar for communicators.

During this third phase, it was the TV news programmes more so than the printed press that took an interest in the figures, with the latter having covered them a year earlier. The survey was spotlighted by TV Globo's *Jornal Hoje*, which reaches a national audience. From then on, the researchers were called in to speak on TV and radio talk shows all across Brazil, riding the momentum of the election campaign climate. By making its way onto television, the campaign had passed a key threshold and was now reaching young audiences. According to the survey, TV is the main source of information for 84.5 per cent of young people in Brazil's metropolitan regions.

NOTES

Introduction

1. The final research reports – one national and eight regional – are available on the Ibase (www.ibase.br) and Pólis (www.polis.org.br) websites.
2. Youth account for approximately 20 per cent of Brazil's total population; of these 34 million young people, 83 per cent live in urban areas and 17 per cent in rural areas.

Chapter 1: Youth and Social Participation in Brazil

1. Belém, Belo Horizonte, Porto Alegre, Recife, Salvador, São Paulo, Rio de Janeiro.
2. In Brazil fundamental education refers to nine years of obligatory schooling for all children between the ages of six and fourteen.
3. These practices constitute an experiment in cultural citizenship that figures as a fourth dimension of citizenship – in addition to the civil, social and political dimensions – and a synthesis of the possibilities open to young people for making public space part of their life experience.

Chapter 2: School and Youth Participation

1. *Juventude Brasileira e Democracia: participação, esferas e políticas públicas* is a national study coordinated by Ibase and Pólis. It was undertaken in seven of Brazil's metropolitan regions and the Federal District to ex-

amine the expectations and real involvement of young people in the public and political spheres and thus broaden debate about participation of young citizens in Brazil. It was also intended that the information generated should influence youth policies at the local, state and national levels. In Belo Horizonte, the study was coordinated by the *Observatório da Juventude* (Youth Observatory) at Minas Gerais Federal University (UFMG) (www.fae.ufmg/objuventude).

2. For a more extensive discussion of the notion of youth see Pais (1993), Margulis (2000), Sposito (2002), Dayrell (2005), and others.

3. From this point on, the figures relate to the opinion poll, which was conducted by probability sampling of a population of 1,000 young people aged 15 to 24, of whom 30.1 per cent were in the 15-17 age group, the same percentage in the 18-20 age group, and 39.8 per cent in the 21-24 age group. The sampling sought a certain homogeneity in terms of sex, that is, 49.6 per cent of the interviewees were male and 50.4 per cent female. Of these, 42.2 per cent were from social class C, 28.1 per cent from social classes D/E and, lastly, 19.8 per cent were from social classes A/B.

4. Of these we should mention Sposito (1993, 1999), Abramo (1994), Caldeira (1984), Minayo (1999), and Abromavay (1999). The same trend is seen among the Portuguese youth studied by Pais (1993) or the Italian youth studied by Cavalli (1997).

5. In the study conducted by *Projeto Juventude* (Abramo 2005), 39 per cent of the young Brazilians never had been to the cinema; 62 per cent had never been to the theatre; 92 per cent had never been to a classical music concert; and most (78 per cent) had never taken part in a public debate or conference (Brenner 2005: 200).

6. The proportion of young people in classes A/B (21.7 per cent) and C (22.3 per cent) who participate is greater than those from social classes D/E (15.7 per cent). Those young people with more schooling tend to participate more (22.9 per cent of those in middle school) than those who have less schooling (16.3 per cent of those who completed fundamental schooling).

7. The young people were asked to say whether they agreed totally, agreed partly, disagreed partly or disagreed totally with the following phrases: 'Most politicians do not represent the interests of the public'; 'Most politicians only work to further their own personal interests'; 'Channels must be opened up for dialogue between citizens and government'; 'People must join together to further their interests' and 'Each person has to look out for their own interests'.

Chapter 3: Youth, Information and Education

1. The aim was to gauge how informed young people were on international politics (Free Trade Area of the Americas – FTAA and United Nations Organisation - UN), social rights (Statute on Children – ECA and quota policies – affirmative action policies) and on organized civil society (World Social Forum, NGOs and Greenpeace).
2. In July 2006, a major newspaper, the *Folha de São Paulo*, reported on an Instituto DataFolha opinion poll on this issue. In this poll 65 per cent of interviewees said they were in favour of adopting quotas for Afro-descendants at public universities. Approval diminished, however, among respondents with higher family income and schooling.
3. In the early 1980s, Brazilian philosopher, José Américo Mota Pessanha, argued emphatically for media to be included in school curricula, beginning in fundamental schooling. In 1997, with the implementation of the National Curricular Parameters, the following transverse themes were incorporated into school curricula: ethics; cultural plurality; environment; health; sexual orientation; work and consumption. The subject of media was not included.

Chapter 4: Debating the Dialogue Methodology

1. Ibase/Pólis, *Relatório Global/ Metodologia/ Diálogos no Brasil*, p. 9.
2. Abramo, Helena Wendel & Branco, Petro Paulo Martoni (eds.) *Retratos da Juventude Brasileira: análises de uma pesquisa nacional*, Instituto Cidadania/Editora Fundação Perseu Abramo (São Paulo, 2005).
3. Regional report, Recife.
4. Regional report, Rio de Janeiro.
5. Regional report, Belo Horizonte.
6. Regional report, Salvador.

Chapter 5: Dialogue Day

1. These two methodological approaches cannot be detailed in the space of this chapter. More information is available on the CD-ROM containing the overall project report (Ibase and Pólis, January, 2006). Please see the report on Dialogue Group Methodology, systematized by Patrícia Lânes.
2. The Dialogue Group is the qualitative methodology used in the survey. The Dialogue Day is the occasion when each group is held. Each day

was conducted by the study teams in the various metropolitan regions and comprised a series of activities and dynamics to encourage interaction among the young people and dialogue among them on the core research questions. The products from the work done on the Dialogue Days provided the input for the qualitative analyses.

3. As pointed out by the São Paulo metropolitan region study team (Corti et al 2005: 89).

4. This article is the product of a multitude of stimulating dialogues: with young people who accepted the invitation to take part in the study; with Marilena Cunha and Alexandre Aguiar, researchers with the Rio de Janeiro team and companions in the adventure of getting young people together and hearing and analyzing their opinions; with Bianca Brandão, the research assistant I talked to for the first time about the expectations surrounding the Dialogue Day; with researchers from the other metropolitan regions and the central team, by way of seminars, reports and an e-forum. My friend, Eliane Ribeiro, from the project's technical team, with whom I have for some years shared views on issues of Brazilian youth, and Névio Fiorin, a member of the Iser Assessoria team, both made valuable contributions to a preliminary draft of this text. My acknowledgements to all of them.

5. The young people's words were taken from the regional reports on the Dialogue Groups that circulated in the study's e-forum. The metropolitan region where the young person took part in the Dialogue is noted in brackets. I was directly involved with the project in Rio de Janeiro, which is why I offer more quotes from what was said there.

6. As rightly noted by the research team in Belém (Silva et al 2005: 80).

7. When the guiding principles behind the Dialogue were set out (listen to people and learn from them; respect different opinions; look for common ground; express disagreement without argument or offence, and so on) (Ibase and Pólis 2006: 7).

8. The authorities, decision-makers in Brazil.

9. (Fischer et al 2005: 135).

10. This aspect was signalled both by the research team in Belo Horizonte, which pointed to the 'lack of settings and channels for participation where these young people can exercise the collective dimension, either in debates or in action' (Dayrell et al 2005: 72), and by the Porto Alegre team, which mentioned the need to set up institutional spaces for listening to young people when formulating public policies directed at that portion of the population (Fischer et al 2005: 135).

11. On the basis of one boy's saying he'd discovered that 'young people are important too', the researchers suggested that 'the opportunity to dialogue with their peers seems, in one way or another, to have reinforced the awareness of "being young"' (De Tommasi 2005: 57).
12. As pointed out by the researchers in São Paulo, 'the young people that made up the public of the Dialogues were from quite different contexts and all that they said and their ways of being and doing bore the imprint of the diversity of youth in the region' (Corti et al 2005: 94).
13. This was also brought out by the survey in Porto Alegre, which indicated that: 'friendship, as a possibility for expanding networks of relations, is strongly emphasized as a fundamental dimension in building youth identities' (Fischer et al 2005: 135).
14. A list of arguments for and against each participation path was presented to the young people in the Dialogue groups as input to their collective thinking.
15. See Oliveira et al (2005: 77).
16. As emphasized by the researchers in the Brasília team: 'the young people perceived the Dialogue Day as an opportunity to talk to each other about important subjects involving politics and citizenship (…), and a fundamentally important space for understanding their role as citizens' (Costa et al 2005: 79).
17. See text on the Dialogue Group Methodology, on the CD-ROM containing the Overall Report (Ibase and Pólis 2006: 3).
18. Ibid, p. 12.
19. Ibid, pp. 3-4.
20. Ibid, p. 11.
21. Freire (1991: 30).
22. Ibid.

Chapter 6: Brazil and Canada: Learning through Collaboration

1. Shor, I., & Freire, P. ' What is the 'Dialogic Method' of Teaching?' *Journal of Education* 169(3), p. 13. (1987)
2. Freire, Paulo, *Pedagogy of the Oppressed*, chapter 3, Continuum International Publishing Group (1970).
3. The dialogue probed ordinary citizens' thinking on the roles and responsibilities and the balance between individual choice, collective need,

market-based solutions and government involvement, using four policy themes: economic development, poverty and social marginalization, environmental and health risks and international development. The results of the national citizens' dialogue on Canada's future are captured in the report *Citizens' Dialogue on Canada's Future: A 21st Century Social Contract,* www.cprn.org

4. CPRN held its national youth dialogue and summit in November 2005 and the research reports *Towards an Action Plan for Canada: Our Vision, Values and Actions* http://www.cprn.org/en/doc.cfm?doc=1435 *Connecting Young People, Policy and Active Citizenship* http://www.cprn.org/en/doc.cfm?doc=1439) - were released in 2006. Both are available on the CPRN Web site.

5. The CPRN team included Mary Pat MacKinnon, Director of the Public Involvement Network, and facilitation expert, Suzanne Taschereau, who was lead facilitator and design expert for several CPRN citizen dialogues. Suzanne in particular also brought considerable international development experience and expertise to the team.

6. For an account of Brazil's successful HIV-AIDS campaign, see Westley, Frances, Zimmerman, Brenda, & Patton, Michael, G*etting to Maybe- How the World is Changed,* chapter 1, pp. 4-6, Random House (Canada, 2006).

7. CPRN's approach to dialogue work also reflects what is sometimes referred to as a 'researcher/practitioner' approach. We are as concerned with and interested in good deliberative processes as we are with policy outcomes.

8. To view the workbooks click on www.cprn.org . Production of these workbooks required considerably more time and resources than other dialogue projects and involved a cross section of CPRN researchers.

9. More information on this research series can be found in *CPRN Network News* Winter 2007 – Number 36 - "The Youth/Ballot Box Disconnect" www.cprn.org

10. For further discussion on this point, see Julia Abelson and Francois-Pierre Gauvin's paper, *Assessing the Impact of Public Involvement: Concepts, Evidence and Policy Implications,* (2006) www.cprn.org

Chapter 7: Networked Research

1. Capoeira is a blend of martial art, game, and dance originating from Brazil, particularly the regions of Bahia, Pernambuco, Rio de Janeiro, Minas Gerais and São Paulo.

INDEX

A

Abramo, Helena 34-35, 79, 188-189
Ação Educativa – Assessoria, Pesquisa e Informação 3, 126, 169, 171-172
access
  to education 32, 47
  to information 7, 40, 63, 113, 124, 170
accountability 96
actors 8, 12, 15, 26, 83-84, 98-99, 140, 147, 150-152, 158, 172
Adorno, Theodor 61, 74
age 4, 17-18, 21-22, 24, 34, 37, 40-41, 45, 65, 188
AIDS 50, 139, 192
alternative media 66, 184
animator 83, 86, 101-103

B

Bendit, René 46
Belo Horizonte Metropolitan Region (BHMR) 32-36, 40 41, 44, 48, 50, 52-53, 174
Bourdieu, Pierre 73-74, 97
Brazil's Statute on Children – ECA 61, 66-69, 71, 189
Brazilian Institute of Geography and Statistics (IBGE) 77
Brazilian Youth and Democracy: Participation, Spheres and Public Policies study 2, 11, 32, 60, 81, 111, 131, 138, 150, 158, 180-181

C

Canadian Policy Research Networks (CPRN) 3, 5, 8, 78, 82, 133-135, 140-148, 156, 158-159, 162-163, 167-168, 192
Carrano, Paulo Cesar 6, 11, 14, 20, 79, 165
Cefaï, Daniel 25

Centro de Referência Integral de Adolescentes (Cria) 3, 126, 175
Chamber of Deputies' Special Commission on Youth 78
Champagne, Patrick 60
Choice Work Dialogue Methodology 3, 7, 79, 124, 155, 158, 161
citizens 26, 43, 51, 79-80, 82-84, 88, 95, 98, 101, 127, 150-151, 181, 183, 188
citizenship 12, 25, 28, 55, 92, 122, 124, 134-135, 166, 168, 170, 175-176, 187, 191-192
civil society organizations 95, 122, 125, 147, 149
class 6, 17-18, 22, 33-34, 39-41, 47-50, 55, 62-65, 69, 72, 103, 113, 141-142, 188
collective
    action 16, 21-22, 25, 27, 43-46, 49, 53, 56, 98-99, 122, 172, 175, 181
    construction method 163
colour 2, 6, 13, 35-36, 40, 63, 65
communication 5, 8-9, 59-60, 64, 67-68, 74, 100, 165-167, 173
    strategies 184
community mobilization 22
Cruz, Rossana 25
cultural
    activities 20-21, 26, 41, 47-48, 50
    animator 103
    expressions 39, 44, 144, 146, 150
    group 39, 46
'cultural citizenship' 25
culture 2-5, 12, 15, 17, 20, 28, 37-41, 48-49, 52, 61, 80-81, 91, 97, 100, 141, 166, 175

D

decentralization 156, 158
decentralized
    approach 143-144
    research 157
    study 161, 163
decision-makers 84, 92-93, 95, 98, 109, 147, 190
deliberation 152
democracy 5, 9, 12, 14, 37, 45, 74, 82, 92, 95, 121-123, 125, 131, 133-134, 138, 147-149, 152-153, 155, 166, 168, 170-171, 174, 179
democratic
    institutions 134
    practice 91, 134, 138, 149-150
    process 51, 83, 91, 146
    system 79
democratization process 179
development 90-100, 155, 166-167, 192
    stakeholders 14-15
'dialogic relationship' 1
Dialogue 3-4, 7-8, 15, 79-85, 87-101, 103, 120, 124, 132, 146, 190-191
    animator 86
    challenges 141
    follow-up studies 84

Dialogue
    Manual 161, 163
    methodology 77, 82, 101, 103, 117, 124, 141-142, 144, 155-156
    process 92-93, 97, 112, 144-146
    Workbook 124, 142
Dialogue Day 4, 80, 84, 94, 98, 101, 105, 109-112, 115-122, 127, 189-191
Dialogue Groups 3, 4, 6-8, 11, 32, 37-39, 42, 50-51, 53-54, 56, 79-80, 84-86, 109-112, 115-118, 125, 127, 160-164, 182, 189, 190-191
    methodology 4, 7, 161, 163, 189, 191
digital
    democracy 40
    inclusion 40, 63
    media 41
dissemination 150, 152, 162, 173
drugs 50, 111

E

education 16, 47, 74, 83
Escola de Formação Quilombo dos Palmares (Equip) 3, 126, 172-173
ethnicity 2, 33-34, 52, 61
evaluation 50, 54, 110-112, 151

F

facilitator 81, 83, 86, 89, 92, 99, 101-103, 109, 114, 124-125, 143, 146-147, 150, 192
Facilitator's Guide 161, 163
Fischer, Nilton 190-191
Fischer, Rosa 60
Free Trade Area of the Americas (FTAA) 61, 66, 68, 71, 189
Freire, Paulo 1, 103, 126-127, 132, 139, 191
fundamental schooling 19, 21, 24, 47-48, 62-63, 188-189

G

gender 2, 6, 13, 21-22, 33-37, 39-41, 50, 52, 55, 170, 176
generational clash 51
globalization 59, 166
Greenpeace 26, 61, 66-68, 71, 189
group participation 18

H

higher education 19, 40, 48-49, 51, 168

I

IBGE (Brazilian Institute of Geography and Statistics) 78
identities 6, 8, 13, 20, 33, 35, 37, 39, 41, 46, 73, 111, 115-117, 191
inequality 12-13, 18, 36, 47, 54-55, 62
information 6, 7, 9, 17-18, 24, 28, 38, 40, 50, 60-68, 71-74, 92, 104, 120, 124, 142, 156, 167-168, 170-172, 177, 180-185, 188
insecurity 39
institutional communication 184
Instituto Brasileiro de Análises Sociais e Economicas (Ibase) 1-2, 32, 34, 82, 101, 103, 157, 160-161, 163-167, 172-173, 177, 184, 187-189, 192
Instituto Cidadania 85
Instituto de Estudos de Formacão e Assessoria em Politicas Sociais (Pólis) 1-2, 78, 125, 131, 153, 156-157, 159, 163-164, 168, 174, 176, 179-180, 188, 192
Instituto de Estudos, Formação e Assessoria em Políticas Sociais (Iser Assessoria) 3, 126, 169, 170, 171, 190
Instituto de Estudos Socioeconômicos (Inesc) 3, 126, 173, 174
Instituto Universidade Popular (Unipop) 3, 126, 176
international partnership 132
International Development Research Center (IDRC) 3, 8, 78, 131, 133, 135, 140, 143-144, 153, 156, 158-159, 163, 167
Internet 40-41, 49, 62-63, 71-72, 164, 183
investigative process 123-126

J

Jobim e Souza, Solange 61, 75

K

Kohlberg, Lawrence 100-101
Krauskopf, Dina 14

L

leadership roles 146
learning 4-5, 8, 15, 17, 45-46, 53, 82, 84, 101, 105, 110-111, 113-114, 117-121, 123-127, 131-133, 138-139, 145-146, 148-149, 150, 153, 168
from practice 126
Leccardi, Carmem 45
leisure 3-4, 16-17, 22-23, 36-39, 41, 46, 48-49, 80-81, 97, 113

M

Margulis, Mário 16, 34, 188

Martins, José de Souza 104

media 5-6, 9, 17, 24, 40-41, 59, 60, 62-70, 73-75, 77-78, 81, 95, 145-146, 148, 150, 152, 162, 164, 166, 169, 180, 183-184, 189

Melucci, Alberto 13, 41, 105

metropolitan regions 2, 7, 11, 62, 79, 85, 89, 105, 109, 115, 118-119, 123, 156, 169, 174, 180-181, 185, 187, 190

middle school 17, 19, 21, 24, 47-49, 62-63, 101, 188

'moral development' 100

Mota Pessanha, José Américo 189

multidisciplinary team 86

N

national networks 149

National Youth Council 15, 78

National Youth Plan 78

National Youth Secretariat 15, 95

network 2-3, 5, 8-9, 26, 39-40, 59, 72, 79, 95, 111, 116, 125, 139-140, 142, 144, 149, 155, 157-161, 163-166, 172-173, 176-177, 191

of reserch partners 3

newspapers 40, 62-65, 67, 71-72, 145, 181, 183-184

North-South cooperation 4

Novaes, Regina 20, 73

O

Observatório da Juventude da Universidade Federal de Minas Gerais 3

Observatório Jovem do Rio de Janeiro 3, 169, 170

opinion
poll 3, 6, 11, 15-16, 18, 32, 34, 83, 109, 160-162, 188-189
survey 24, 97

outreach of results 145

P

participation 2-4, 6, 11-12, 16-18, 20-23, 25, 27-29, 31-32, 34-35, 38-39, 41-48, 50-56, 60, 65, 78-80, 86-91, 94, 96-101, 121-123, 126-127, 134, 138, 144, 147-148, 151, 155-156, 162, 164, 166, 170, 173, 179, 181-184, 188, 190-191

in social movements 21

in the public sphere 96-97, 121

in the school 47

party youth organizations 53

Peralva, Angelina 33

perceptions 3, 7-8, 23, 34, 42-43, 46, 93, 156

Piaget, Jean 90, 100

policy
  makers 15, 27, 81, 104-105, 147, 150, 179, 185
  outcomes 140, 192
  research 149, 151

Pólis (Instituto de Estudos de Formacão e Assessoria em Politicas Sociais) 1-2, 78, 125, 131, 153, 156-157, 159, 163-164, 168, 174, 176, 179-180, 188, 192

political participation 12, 16, 23, 25, 31, 42-44, 46, 56, 78, 94, 148

poor youth 2, 17-18, 48, 63, 142

popular education 103, 109-110, 125-127

poverty 39, 96, 134, 192

press 5, 8-9, 180-185
  advisors 179, 181, 184
  campaign 179-180, 182
  release 181, 185
  summary 181

programmes 15, 95, 122, 162, 169

public
  engagement 149, 152
  policies 13-15, 26, 28, 55, 66, 74, 77, 81-84, 87, 93-94, 98, 104, 134, 166, 168, 174, 177, 179, 182, 190

Q

qualitative
  research 97
  study 3, 109

quantitative study 47, 160

R

race 6, 35, 37, 40, 50, 52, 55, 61

radio 40, 62, 64, 67, 72, 145, 183-185

Redes e Juventudes (Recife) 126

regional networks 144, 149

religion 2, 20, 35, 41

research reports 128, 187, 192

researchers 3, 5, 25, 81, 83, 88, 90, 94-95, 97, 109-110, 114, 117-118, 123-124, 126-127, 132, 139, 143-144, 149-150, 152, 159, 161, 167, 171, 177, 183-185, 190-192

Ribes, Rita 61

S

Salgado, Raquel 61

Santos, Milton 13

school 6, 17-18, 19, 22, 27, 32, 34, 37-38, 40, 44, 46-50, 52-54, 56, 64, 66, 73, 84, 97, 110, 112, 115, 117, 119, 127, 169
  at the weekends 52

schooling 17-19, 41, 49, 62-63
sex 18, 61, 63, 65, 188
sexuality 35, 50
sociability 26-27, 37-39, 50, 110
social
 class 2, 4, 13, 18, 22, 36, 40, 61, 66, 90, 188
 inclusion 5
 movements 21, 42, 52, 69-70, 80, 99, 104, 122, 126, 167, 170, 185
 networks 47, 56, 115
'social moratorium' 16
Sposito, Marilia 14, 41, 46, 79, 188
stakeholders 14-15, 28, 43, 168
State 12, 99, 122
statistical survey 3
Strategic communications 145
survey 3, 12, 16, 22-24, 28, 39, 47, 49, 51, 53, 55, 64, 97, 109

T

television (TV) 6-7, 40, 59-64, 66-67, 71-74, 145, 183-185
'television habit' 74
tertiary education 51

U

unemployment 17, 37, 54
United Nations Organization (UN) 61, 66, 68, 71-72, 189
universal access to education 47
Universidade Federal de Minas Gerais (UFMG) 126, 174, 188
Universidade Federal do Rio Grande do Sul (UFRGS) 3, 126, 168
Universidade Federal Fluminense (UFF) 126, 170
Urresti, Marcelo 16

V

violence 13-14, 27, 39, 50, 55, 88, 105, 152

W

Workbook 124, 142, 144, 146, 192
World Social Forum 61, 66-68, 70-71, 158, 160, 162, 164, 166, 189

Y

young people 2-8, 11-28, 31-57, 60-74, 78, 80, 83-85, 88-89, 91-105, 109-128, 131-135, 138, 145-150, 152, 160, 162, 169-170, 172, 174, 175-176, 179, 181-185, 187-192

youth 1-2, 5-7, 9, 11-20, 22-28, 32-40, 44-48, 50, 52-56, 62-64, 66, 69, 73, 77-80, 82, 85-86, 88, 90, 92-93, 98, 100, 104-105, 109, 115-116, 121-124, 126-128, 133-134, 138-139, 141-151, 168-175, 177, 179, 183-185, 188, 190, 192
and democracy 82, 131, 134, 149, 179
citizenship 28
condition 33-37, 39, 47, 50, 171, 175

youth
culture groups 20, 52
groups 15, 25, 27, 39, 80, 100, 170, 172
participation 6, 12, 16-18, 28, 31-32, 35, 44-45, 47-48, 50, 52-53, 55-56, 79, 122, 134, 138, 173
policies 9, 11, 13-15, 41, 172-173, 188
policy makers 15
unemployment 36